RUN FOR YOUR LIFE

RUN FOR YOUR LIFE

From Victim to Victor

DENAIR MARIE

HARRIS AUTHOR SERVICES
Worldwide

Run for Your Life: From Victim to Victor
by Denair Marie
(Third Edition)

ISBN (Print): 978-0-692-67188-7
ISBN (eBook): 978-0-692-67189-4

www.harrisauthorservices.com

Contents

From My Heart to Yours

I absolutely *love* books! I also love connecting with people. I am driven by making real connections with people with the hopes of building lasting bonds and making this world a better place through positive relationships.

While I have shared so much of myself in this book, I still feel like our connection is limited by black and white static pages. As such, I would like you to **go to my website www.denairmarie.com** to experience pictures, audio, video, and other living content that connects my *story* with Denair, the real person.

I cannot wait to see you there!

Dedication

I dedicate this book to my mother, Mary Jane Felder. I am who I am because of who she is.

She is, without a doubt, the strongest, most dedicated, and most God fearing person I know. Her faith is unwavering.

When I was younger, I did not want to be as giving and caring as she, because it was and continues to be her whole world. I did not understand her strength in staying with my dad, and then I became her. I became Mary.

My mom began this very same journey of helping abused women almost 20 years ago before she got stabbed over 60 times, trying to rescue someone and became his victim.

My passion for empowering women began with rescuing my mom. When I was a child I had no voice, but now I've grown to be a woman that would change the lives of millions. I didn't understand it until I wrote this book and began to tell *my* story.

Mommy, thank you for handing me the baton. With God's help, we can help many more people move from *Victim to Victor.*

I Love you, mommy! You are my *she*-ro!

Special Thanks

"Though no one can go back and make a brand new start, anyone can start from now and make a brand new ending." —Carl Bard

I would like to thank my big brother, **Edward E. Felder, Jr.** (aka *the Funding Guy*, whom I officially knighted, *the Writing Guy*). Thanks Ed for helping me create a brand new ending.

The journey of writing this book was one of the most difficult challenges I have ever experienced. Ed helped me birth a world of creativity and brought my story to life. Ed displayed an exceptional gift for extracting joy, pain, tragedy, comedy and adventure from each session, reviving victories and defeats, then making them dance on paper like exquisite calligraphy.

I appreciate the countless hours he sacrificed interviewing me, writing with me, and crying with me as he learned about so many horrific details of my life, which on many occasions, almost broke him down. He selflessly researched a topic that is gruesome, unpopular, and taboo for most men to stomach, all while demonstrating professionalism and great skill as a writer and coach.

When I was too overwhelmed by the daunting memories that

plagued me day and night, Ed comforted me and continued to push me through the pain. He would say, "Come on, Denair! We are almost there. The world needs this story." He gave me many ideas to propel my project and make it the best it could be.

If you have a story you are yearning to bless the world with, no matter how painful, embarrassing, hilarious, or all of the above, Ed is your guy. He can help make your dream of becoming an amazing author come true and also help you create a brand new ending.

Thank you, Ed for being my brother, mentor, confidant, and friend.

With love,

Your baby sister, Denair Marie

From My Brother, Edward Felder, Jr.

The vulgarity of what she'd just whispered forced me to doubt who she really was! I cringed, but she continued. I was embarrassed to listen.

I was a man. I was heartbroken. I was filled with rage; a rage that would easily allow a quiet guy like me, who attended two Christian universities, to snap a guy's neck and not flinch afterward. I was in a fog. I could barely hold my head up as she broke down and shared how she was violently slapped, choked, and thrown around for years.

I showed her how to tie her shoelaces when she was 16 months old. I watched her like a hawk in elementary school as she danced through the halls. In high school, I taught her how to play spades, helped her with her algebra, and boasted that she was the prettiest girl around. I doubled-dared my homies to approach her.

There was no one closer to her in this world than I, her big brother. That's what I believed when I escorted her from our ninth floor apartment in the most violent housing projects in America to one of the most breathtaking college campuses on

God's green earth. I smiled. I did well. I'd protected her. I taught her to trust her instincts. I repeatedly told her she was royalty.

What she failed to tell me, until she and I began to pen her memoir, was how she was strangled to death and later revived. It was 15 years earlier when she had been a victim of domestic violence on a daily basis for nearly nine and one-half years.

I fell prostrate. It was frightening to learn the extent of her physical and mental abuse. It was embarrassing to learn she had to concoct an elaborate ruse and flee 500 miles to begin a new life with her head on a swivel, always watching her back. I felt like an idiot for not knowing. I taught her everything, *besides* how to speak up! Why didn't she just speak up?

Then it dawned on me. It was my responsibility to check on my baby sister and ask her the right questions. Truth is, no woman should ever have to run for their lives or flinch and duck for cover. Shame on us if we wait until one of our football heroes is under the spotlight and caught on video, abusing a woman before we stand up and say, "Enough is enough!"

Rather than forcing them to run for their lives, gentlemen we should be running to their rescue. I pray that *Run for Your Life*, this riveting story of survival, inspires you to run and hug your daughter, speak kinder words to your wife, check on your aunties, and build a community of men who say, "I am stronger. I am wiser. I am better. I *am* my sister's keeper. She shall run no more!

Denair "Extraordinaire" Felder, you're my hero. You've taught me what strength really is! —**Edward E. Felder, Jr. MBA**

From My Brother, Thomas Felder

This book contains snapshots, memories, and experiences of a survivor of domestic violence. Denair is a hero to so many survivors of abuse. I applaud her courage in sharing her story, as it will empower others to share their stories and shed their hurt, shame, and fear. As she beautifully captured the courage of going forward even when life gives you a setback, she has provided us a roadmap for surviving adversity without becoming bitter and broken.

It is time for us to shed light on domestic violence because it can only thrive in the dark. I am thankful for Denair's passion and strength, and grateful to God that she has taken what was designed to destroy her and used the lessons of her experiences to help others.

I have known her all my life. She is my sister and my best friend. It was not until I read this book that I began to understand her struggle. I recommend that all men read it, not just women. Domestic violence is not only a women's issue, but it is also an issue, which affects us all. Denair, I thank you for reminding us that, "It is not over 'til we win." —**Thomas Felder**

FROM MY BROTHER, THOMAS FELDER

From My Son, Shon D. Huggins, Jr.

Arguably the most memorable night I have ever had was one Friday in 1997, during the middle of my second grade school year. I was seven years old that year, but I will never forget how that day shifted my faith, fears, goals, and achievements forever.

Just two days prior, Wednesday evening, my mother shared with my sister and me that we would be spending the next few days at my cousin Veronica's home, with my cousins Daevon, Justin, and Naquasha. I cannot speak for my sister, but I always loved heading to my cousin's home because they had a *Nintendo*. We would boil franks and blanket them with bread, ketchup, and mustard while playing video games all night long. I thought it was a great idea, and until Sunday evening, it was an ideal weekend with the family.

That evening I overheard my mother speaking to Veronica. "I'm on the way to pick up the kids," she said. Oddly, I was confused when my mother pulled up to the curb in a *U-Haul* truck. When she exited the truck, she thanked Veronica for watching us, and with tears in her eyes shared with my sister and me that we were leaving my father, our home, New York, and our lives behind.

I'm not one for tears, and I can't remember if I cried any as we drove through the night to Maryland, but I vividly remember hearing my sister Denika's painful sobs as I lay between a bag of clothes and my bicycle behind the front seats (there were only two seats in the truck). The following Monday I don't recall thinking too much about my abrupt change in life; the school I thought I would attend in Maryland had a bike rack full of bikes in the front of the building. I was ecstatic at the thought of riding my bicycle to school.

I guess there was an ominous air that something major was coming in our household. In my opinion, my family had the perfectly balanced structure. I viewed my father as the disciplinarian. No matter how tired the family was, he had our clothes pressed, and on Sabbath mornings, he rounded us all up and got us to church without fail. If I was disobedient, my mother and father would rationally talk to me about it, showing me the error in my decision, then my father would say, "Son, this is going to hurt me more than it hurts you, but you must be disciplined for your disobedience," and he would pull down my pants, lay me over his lap, and lay *heavy licks* on my backside.

Now, my mother was no pacifist in by any means, but there was trust between my parents that they could assume balanced roles in the household and raise a proper family. They both disciplined me, and they both showed me tender love, but my mother was always undoubtedly my comforter. She would read to my sister and me nightly. She would take us to school daily and send us off with kisses. She was as endearing as anyone could ask, but things began to shift, and as I reflect upon it now, I witnessed a lioness take on the king of the pride with indomitable strength.

At the time, I didn't know, but my father had picked up a drug habit that changed the normalcy in our home. I started to see unflushed cigarette butts in our toilet when I went to the bathroom. I vividly remember a night when my father was clearly intoxicated, and my mother didn't want him to take the car, for fear him being killed while driving under the influence. I awoke out of my sleep to the sounds of their wrestling in the living room. I got up and went the living room to witness my father's masculine frame towering over my mother trying to grab the car keys. "Shon, go back to bed!" she yelled as she continued fending off my father. They struggled for a long time, and I just stood and watched. I couldn't move. Words can't describe the anguish of that moment. There were other times my mother changed the locks hoping to keep my father away for the safety of our family, but *that* didn't end well either. There were instances when, like the *Big Bad Wolf*, my father literally tried to break down the door, and again I stood there near the entrance of the kitchen watching my mother in tears as she bunkered her back against the apartment door, some time after midnight, screaming for my father to leave before he woke my sister and me, or the neighbors. Once they were both arrested for fighting! I can't shake the image of stretched out t-shirt necklines and the cut faces of my parents being put into the cop car as the lights flashed against the walls of our city building like Christmas lights. We made attempts to leave, by way of different relatives throughout New York City, but with no success.

In all the madness before we left New York, though unusual, I still loved my parents very much and could not imagine life without either of them. My grades never dropped below a "B+," and I was still completely obedient to both of my parents, sometimes confused about whom I should obey when they gave me conflicting instructions towards the end of our time together.

Until recently, I selfishly thought that my sister and I were the only ones who suffered because of the divorce and abrupt separation of our family. I suffered, in many ways, mostly reflecting in my education. I simply wouldn't do my work resulting in my first "C," then my first "D." I eventually began to fail classes for the first time. Luckily I was never left behind because my teachers knew I had the knowledge and comprehension.

The negative effects on my sister's life could be clearly seen in her social decision-making habits. Her grades never suffered. In fact, she continued to be a star student, and with tears in her eyes would argue the teacher down about receiving a "B" in class until the grade was changed to an "A." I always admired her for that. She even graduated college with honors through her pregnancy with my favorite niece, De'Amor. It was outside of my sister's academic life that her friends influenced her to behave in ways that were contrary to our upbringing.

In my recent adulthood, I have come to the realization that, like my sister and I, the divorce also had residual effects on my parents. My father dove further into his addiction without the presence of his family, whom he most certainly loved. It took more than a decade for him to overcome and find a new purpose.

My mother now had the struggles of being a single mother with an unstable income, unstable living situation, and unstable children. Each of our foundations had been shaken. We all had to learn how to live all over again with our new impediments.

Each of us were something like stroke patients in rehab, learning how to use our limbs again and redeveloping our speech because none of us talked about it. We just struggled individually in silence, resulting in unhealthy romantic relationships, poor decision-making, and contemplation of suicide. I could feel everyone's pain, but we were always so good at putting on our best faces for the outside world! These were indeed tough times, but there was a diamond that was revealed due to this tremendous pressure.

Our story is a one of overcoming obstacles. Second to God Almighty, Denair Marie Huggins is the MVP and All-Star of this story. If my mother were to write a "How-to" book, I would advocate the title, "How to Create a Sense of Urgency." You will see throughout this book how many mistakes each party made, but unlike most people who wallow in depression, my mother always had a sense of urgency to push through the valley of pain and emerged to ascend the highest peaks in her life. At times, my mother worked three jobs to maintain a high-quality of life for my sister and I. I have seen her humble herself before less qualified people in work situations, because she refused to jeopardize her income that provided for us, no matter what. My mother has survived deadly domestic violence situations! She even survived the scorn of ungrateful and unappreciative offspring. She's a warrior!

Everyone who ever walked this earth has faced defining moments of betrayal, pain, and pressure. These moments can either destroy us or teach us perseverance! Everyone goes through these things at some time or the other, but not everyone makes a conscious decision to succeed at all costs. This is a story of success from someone who leaves an indelible impression on everyone she engages. Pay close attention and learn what it takes to succeed at all costs! —**Shon D. Huggins, Jr.**

Disclaimer

This is the story of some of my life events, which I recollect and am sharing with you. This account of the details is subjective. Others who were also involved in some of these events probably have varying recollections of the same events. As you may know, this is the case with all of our memories surrounding significant, traumatic, or joyful life events. I have done my best to be faithful to the facts along with my thoughts and feelings about those facts.

I have changed the names of some and kept the names of others, depending on the situation, to preserve anonymity where I deemed necessary to do so.

My singular purpose for sharing some of my deepest thoughts and feelings in this book is to provide support, empowerment, and encouragement to anyone who may have had similar experiences to mine. It is not my intention to berate, demean, or otherwise cast aspersion upon anyone. However, facts are facts, and I have been faithful to the facts as I see them.

Enjoy.

1

Death by Strangulation

Dear God,

The boils are so painful on my feet

They are swollen bloody, and blistering

It feels like I'm walking on glass and hot coals

Deformed flesh hanging off my bones

Filled with fluid

Achilles is inflamed

I'm exhausted and tired

from running...

My journey to see the end is relentless

I have the mindset that says I

believe in myself and will see

this to the end but I'm weary

This is called commitment.

I've been training

I put in hours of sacrifice

My grueling preparation

allowed me to endure joint pain

My discipline born in adversity

Running is a one-woman sport but I need your help

I can't make it alone!

Don't you hear me, God?

Don't you see my pain?

Can you still hear my prayers?

I'm tired of complaining

No stories of bad knees

I can't blame anyone if I lose

I must put on my survivor mask

You look at me and don't know what I've been through

Like me, there are other survivors of abuse

You don't see the scars...not the mental ones anyway

My back is aching

It feels like I'm carrying two humongous boulders

My ankles are swollen

I can't stand up straight...but

There is no give up in me

And I will fight to ignore that

voice in my head that keeps

saying..."Shut up and die, Denair! Just shut up and die!"

Rick repeatedly screamed, "I'm not going back to jail, I can't go back to jail!" He said, "You brought this foolishness on yourself. You didn't have to die tonight! This is all your fault. Are you happy now?"

"Am I hearing him correctly? When was Rick ever in jail?" My attempt at shouting "Get off of me," barely trickled out as a whisper.

There was no reasoning with Rick.

Who was this person? I didn't recognize Rick at all. He was harsh and deliberate. He was emotionless. He wasn't scared, just dripping with evil and evil intentions. Where did this person come from? This wasn't the Rick that I dated for the last nine months. His murdering me would be swift and intentional.

"Die? Die? I can't die now!"

Lovie, my two-year-old granddaughter will never know the amazing plans I had for her. I had such big plans for Lovie and me. We'd go on weekly shopping excursions in New York and Atlanta during her teenage years. I'd teach her how to style hair just like I taught her mother. Because of Rick, it now appeared that my future with Lovie would be vaporized.

In my mind, I fought with everything in me to live but Rick's years of martial arts training and competitive fighting put me at a distinct disadvantage. This *ex-boyfriend* of mine was deranged and seemingly out of his mind.

I tried pleading, twisting, and kneeing, all to no avail. I was literally cemented under the weight of his 260-pound frame. My arms were pinned so tightly under him there was no chance of me punching, elbowing, or scratching myself free.

There was no time to think; everything was happening so fast. Okay, my next move, maybe I'd free myself by angling my head toward his left forearm. I struggled to bite him, and I figured I'd at least scar him for life, and if I didn't make it out of this situation, the *CSI* would be able to piece the story together. Thankfully, following the bite, Rick slightly released his python-like hold on my neck. I was able to take a short breath for a second, praying I could survive this ordeal.

He quickly recovered and tripled his efforts to choke the life out of me.

In my mind, I was fighting, but I had nothing left. I could feel the life being squeezed out of me. My mouth was so dry, and I could not hear anything. Were my senses leaving me too? Had I missed the chance to scream for my neighbors? And what happened to the contractors who were working on my home for the last eight hours? Is this a bad dream that I'm trapped in?

"Lord please let Tony and Roscoe still be downstairs. Save me Lord. Let them hear my muted cry!!! Allow them to sense my danger!"

There was so much pressure applied to my weary frame; it was a miracle that I was still hanging on. Rick snatched the back of my neck with such force that it seemed as if this was it.

I was floating in and out of consciousness, trying to avoid the inevitable.

I never imagined death could be so painful. As I struggled to breathe my last breath, I'd come to the realization that this rainy Saturday evening, just seven days after celebrating my 42nd birthday, would be my last night on earth.

I'd survived growing up in the notorious Webster Avenue Housing Projects in the South Bronx, being homeless, a number of life-threatening health challenges, and I wasn't going to give now! But was this my time? My mind fought against it all ending that night.

He outweighed me by 120 pounds, and his six-foot, two-inch frame made it difficult for me to gain any leverage. I was tossed around like a rag doll. I was on a physical and emotional roller coaster.

Despite all the years of standing up to bullies and defending myself, I was helpless against him. He was dead-set on ending my life, and there was absolutely nothing I could do about it.

As tears flowed down the side of my face, my mind quickly replayed the events that took place in the months and weeks leading up to this horrific day.

I began by asking myself, "How could such an exciting day spiral so out of control?" "How did I miss the signs of his pending rage?"

I'd broken up with Rick for the fifth and final time the prior Saturday and asked that he no longer call, text, or stop by my office. I told him my brother Tommy would be heading to Europe in the next few days, and I would be overwhelmed running the law practice for the next few weeks. I would have no down time for drama or to entertain his calls discussing my decision.

I can even recall exiting the mall one day. I said, "Tommy, I have an eerie feeling I'm being watched." Tommy would say something like, "You're tripping, let's keep it moving." There were other times too, but I'd tell myself it was all those years of having to look over my shoulder. It was an era when girls would steal coats and bags from each other for status. Also, when you could lose your life over a link chain or less. Nope, this was not called paranoid—just plain old survival.

During my initial courtship, it was flattering that Rick was popping in on me at the office to drop off either a dozen roses for me and *Chipotle* or Pizza for the staff. I adored the efforts of his willingness to show me how he felt about me along with his nice little gifts.

I thought to myself, "Isn't this sweet?" Every lady wants to be swept off her feet and charmed. While the office receptionist and admin staff would be excited to have takeout delivered free of charge, Rick's unannounced visits just didn't sit right with me.

My girlfriends would explain away my uneasiness by saying he's just improvising. They'd tell me I'm a workaholic with *zero* social life. They'd say, Enjoy the moment. Don't over-think things." They'd further put me on blast by saying, "You're too picky, you never date, you never take lunch." In a sense they were right. I was regularly asked on dates by professional athletes, attorneys, doctors and high profile politicians who stopped by the office, did business with our title company, or retained our law practice to handle some big merger or real estate development.

No matter how tall, dark or handsome the guy was, my answer was always the same: "I'm flattered, but right now the timing just isn't the best." I'd politely tell them, "My plate is full with work, finishing my degree, and traveling the state training single moms how to successfully enter the workforce."

It wasn't that I didn't like going out and meeting new and interesting people. My entire life I'd always been a social butterfly. I had grown up in a household with seven people, and it wasn't uncommon for my family to entertain up to 30 guests two to three weekends per month.

It's just that with the hectic schedule I had, the two or three hours I wasn't working or studying I'd prefer to engage in something called sleep. I was literally running on fumes and sleep for me was a luxury I couldn't continue to ignore.

"Why not give Rick a chance? Why not give Rick a chance? Why not give Rick a chance?!" I quickly found myself lobbying for Rick. My girls Veronica, Nicole, and Cynthia, who had become his chief advocates, were rubbing off on me.

Maybe Rick was popping up unannounced because I was too busy in the office and I failed to notice when he called me on my cellphone.

While I tried explaining away his sudden visits to the firm, after a while there was no getting around the fact I felt like a suspect being grilled on an episode of *Law and Order* whenever I did pick up his calls. One moment he was warm and soothing and the next he would be extremely abrasive claiming my alibi didn't quite fit the timeline.

In my mind, I could hear him saying, "Your Honor, permission to treat the witness as hostile," as I often explained to Rick my 14 to 15 hour work days, coupled with the three to five hours I spent each evening completing course work for my degree in criminal justice. My schedule was taking a toll on my health and our relationship.

Surprisingly, Rick took the news of our breakup quite well. He was in agreement that we needed to clear our heads and our hearts and step away from our nine-month courtship.

What a relief!

The truth of the matter was Rick was extremely controlling. I was 24 hours away from my birthday, and I couldn't imagine spending another nine minutes, nine days or nine months calling him my boo. I refused to start another year with him by my side.

Rick wanted to know the Who, What, Where, and Why of every little step I took. An example of one of our calls would go something like:

> *Rick: Denair are you still at the mall? It's 10:01 p.m. The stores are closed and who actually shops this late?*
>
> *Me: Rick, yes, I'm still shopping. Macys is having a one-night sale for their VIP customers.*
>
> *Rick: Oh, okay! You should have told me. I would love to have gone with you. By the way, your car is in your office parking lot. Who did you ride with? How did you get there?*
>
> *Me: I'm with my brother, Tommy. He's driving.*
>
> *Rick: Oh okay! I just missed you and wanted to know you were okay.*

Rick's concerns had a hint of hostility. Although slightly humorous at the time, I could see where our shaky relationship was heading, and I wanted no part of it anymore. It was exhausting always trying to explain my whereabouts. My life wasn't complicated. I was either at work, school, shopping, or church.

I finally told myself enough is enough. I was tired of always being accused. The interrogations that were masked as simple conversations had to end. In the nine months, we *dated* we went out fewer than 12 times, although our lack of going out probably had a lot to do with my rigorous schedule. Thinking back, subconsciously, I most likely held back due to his unrelenting questioning and controlling nature.

A trip to the *Cheesecake Factory* to grab a bite to eat, a walk in the park, or maybe catch the latest blockbuster made up the bulk of the time we spent together. It really didn't make a difference what we saw, whether the latest romance or laugh out loud comedy, I'd always fall asleep, sometimes before the opening credits.

I was beginning to feel like a prisoner in my own skin. I hadn't signed up for this version of *Love Connection*!

So when Rick agreed to my recommendation that we'd part ways on amicable terms, it was music to my ears. It was none of that back and forth. The tune playing wasn't Heather Headly's song, *In My Mind, I'd Always be His Lady*.

Nope, it was more like Vivian Green's hit, *Gotta Go, Gotta Leave*! The passionate words she sang echoed in my mind:

> *I gotta go. I gotta leave.*
>
> *So please don't make it hard for me.*

I've given enough, I'm tired of love,

I gotta let it go.

After the draining inquisitions, I'd endured those past few months it was refreshing to kick back and enjoy a stress-free Sunday.

Ironically, of all the places I could have gone on my first day as a single lady, I found myself in isle 11 at the *Home Depot*!

That's right! I had no time for *pity or passion parties.* The only guy I wanted to hear from was Frank Wright. Frank was my 68-year-old associate who was helping me select custom granite, new light fixtures, and materials for my soon-to-be California Closet.

While most girls secretly hoped to be proposed to by their prince charming, I know for a fact every girl dreamed of having a huge California Closet.

In seven days I'd have my dream closet built, and the thought of that had me dancing down the aisles of the store that proclaimed, "YOU can do it! We can help!"

After four hours of shopping bliss, I bid my regal sales associate adieu. I circled back around to my condo to meet up with the contractor.

While scrambling to straighten up the kitchen before he'd arrived, I'd received a surprising call from an elderly guy who came highly recommended. Was I missing something? I asked him to repeat what he just said... and again he uttered, "Ms. Huggins, I won't be able to install your granite countertops as promised." Dismayed, I pressed the contractor on why he was turning down the opportunity to do my kitchen and bathroom.

He said, "Ma'am in all of my 40 years of work, I'd never received such negative vibes from a client." Completely unaware of what he was referring to, my mouth hung open as he continued. He went on to say that my *husband* shot him such an awful and vile look, that he felt threatened the remainder of the evening.

Embarrassed that I was involved with someone so evil, I apologized profusely before ending our conversation. I wanted to shout to Mr. Wright that the idiot wasn't my husband, but what good would that do?

I was so flabbergasted by what I'd just heard; I couldn't muster the energy to write the two papers I was supposed to turn in by midnight. Disappointed and disgusted beyond belief, I headed to bed hours earlier than I had in a long time.

My only solace was knowing Rick and I were finally done. Good riddance!

By midafternoon the next day (Monday), I'd been so inundated with filing bankruptcies and piecing together land development deals that I didn't have time to focus on any more of Rick's insane baggage.

As I wrapped up my day around 9 p.m., I'd noticed there were nearly a dozen yellow sticky messages plastered over my desk. Not surprising, each message was from Rick requesting that I call him immediately. I checked my cell phone only to learn Rick had texted me 10 times asking me to join him for dinner that evening.

Twenty-two messages in a single day. There was no crisis or fire to put out. Rick was simply being Rick. I rolled my eyes, selected *delete all*, and kept it moving.

Tuesday, I spent the entire day meeting with our newest client, Prince Georges County, one of the wealthiest counties's in the United States. Tommy, my astute brother, had outdone himself landing this prestigious account. With Tommy heading out of the country for the next few weeks, it would be my responsibility to give the red carpet treatment to our distinguished new client.

As I reached into my bag to convert my cell phone from vibrate to my favorite ringtone, I noticed I had 25 missed calls from Rick.

This was insane! Rick was more harassing and relentless than I'd ever imagined. I tried putting an end to this madness by blocking his number. However, my current cellular carrier did not have that technology at the time. I was advised to check back in a few months. My only other option was to change my cell phone number altogether. When I ran this by Tommy, he reminded me that too many of our clients had my number, and this was not a good time with them not being able to have access to him for the next few weeks. So much for our amicable break-up!

By the end of the day on Friday, there were 80 more missed calls from Rick and dozens of colored stickies on my desk, door, and computer.

Any guilt or ill feelings I harbored for ending things with Rick had evaporated. I'd regretted the day I met him, with his corny lines and opening my car door for me. Hmmm, must have been acting. As I lay in bed that Friday evening trying to wind down, there was a tightening in my stomach that kept me tossing and turning.

I had no time for Rick's foolishness. I would be in complete overdrive and needed to remain laser sharp, and razor focused. Tommy was headed for Europe tomorrow, and the pressure was really on to make certain the practice didn't miss a beat. I'd have triple the workload and wouldn't have the energy to deal with Rick's tantrums.

As I closed my eyes, my final thoughts were that I just needed his unnecessary drama to end!

I awoke Saturday with such great joy and happiness in my heart. I found myself humming then bellowing a powerful hymn by Pastor Charles Jenkins. Music has always been a great comfort to me. I can count on it for solace and relief day or night; especially on the Sabbath.

My God is Awesome!

He can move mountains

Keep me in the valley

Hide me from the rain

My God is Awesome!

Heals me when I'm broken

Strength where I've been weakened

Forever, he will reign!

My God is Awesome!

I kicked the sheets off and bounced out of bed. Although it was drizzling outside, there was *sunshine in my soul today*. There were no thoughts of Rick or the misery he'd put me through.

This Saturday would be the best Saturday ever! Since I was a little girl, Saturdays were always my favorite. I'd rejoice the moment I opened my eyes.

My love and excitement of Saturdays was comparable to a kid on Christmas morning. There was always a newness and fresh feeling in the air.

My earliest memories of Sabbath include being dressed in my finest dress, my hair was done in two French braids, and black patent leather shoes. My siblings and I would sing songs of praise such as *This Little Light of Mine* and *Father Abraham* during the ride to church in Dad's car.

Upon walking into church I would be greeted with hugs and kisses from 40 of my best friends who all just happened to be my first cousins. We'd share stories from the past week, swap snacks, and keep from getting caught whispering in church. The really fun parts of church included performing in plays, listening to amazing Bible stories, and performing in the kiddie choir for divine worship.

On this Saturday morning, as I was getting dressed for church, I was acting as my own minister of music and praise team leader. I was remixing *Take the Shackles Off My Feet So I Can Dance*, by Mary Mary with a little *Praise Is What I Do*, by Pastor William Murphy.

I was having a Hallelujah good time in the Lord.

Yes, this was the day that the Lord had made, and I would rejoice and be glad in it. There would be no outside distractions.

By the time I entered the doors of Restoration Praise Church in Bowie, Maryland, I'd already experienced my blessing, and I had the smile on my face to prove it. I was intent on squeezing my joy into the first, second, and third person I'd came in contact with.

It was 7:30 a.m. and I was excited about joining my childhood friends from New York, and former classmates from Oakwood University, prepare and deliver peanut butter & jelly and bologna & cheese sandwiches for the scores of homeless men and women who slept on park benches in downtown Washington, D.C.

I took great pride in being a contributor to this amazing ministry. I happily rolled up my sleeves, kicked off my heels and began placing potato chips, granola bars, apples, and juice boxes into small brown paper bags.

But for the grace of God, I might be homeless and hungry again.

In the midst of reminiscing about my college days and singing songs of praise, I decided to call my baby brother and see whether he'd made the first leg of his flight to Europe.

As I powered on my cell phone, I received an urgent call from my primary contractor, Tony. The fact that he was talking a mile a minute, coupled with the lousy reception in the kitchen, only allowed me to catch every third word he was saying.

Although, he said, he'd call back in a second. The gist of his call was to tell me I needed to head home immediately. From what I could make out, there was a terrible storm hitting our area shortly. If he didn't unload the material for my California Closet within the next 30 minutes every item would be ruined and non-refundable.

One of my greatest joys of attending Restoration Praise Church was listening to my childhood friend, Pastor Paul Graham. His manner of storytelling was so vivid and down to earth that he made every story in the Old Testament seem relevant and vital to my daily life. I hated leaving early, especially on a day I was expected to serve, but I couldn't afford to waste thousands of dollars in material.

Maybe I'd hit the Internet and catch the sermon on *PraizeVision*. Yes, that's exactly what I'd do.

Before hopping into my car I ran into Pastor Graham's wife, Windy and told her I wanted to start a clothing and shoe ministry for single moms or women in need corporate attire. I mentioned I'd reach out to her during the week to discuss the particulars.

Although it was only noon, the sky was already getting dark. Guilty for having a lead foot even in heels, I applied just a little more pressure on the gas pedal, trying to avoid the dozens of speeds traps on my route.

Six blocks away from my condo, the phone rang. As I prepared to blurt out, "Tony I'm just down the road!" I was startled to hear Rick's voice with the first words out of his mouth, "WHERE ARE YOU?" followed by, "ARE YOU AT CHURCH?" My mind answered by saying, "Really, what is it to you and why are you calling me?" but my mouth said, "No I am going home to open the door for my contractors." From the tone of my voice, he sensed my tension and quickly shifted the questioning to: "Are you giving out food to the homeless this afternoon?" *Mr. Q&A* had a gift for skillfully switching the subject when he knew I was reaching my boiling point. Hip to his game, I simply told Rick, "This interrogation is over," and calmly hung up the phone.

In the three minutes it took to get to my condo, Rick called my phone, back to back to back at least five consecutive times. On this Saturday afternoon, I said, "No weapon formed against me shall prosper." Nope! This phone stalker wasn't going to steal my joy; not when I'd have my California Closet shortly, or at least the materials in my possession.

I simply powered off my phone. Headache eliminated!

Was this guy for real? For someone who claimed they never knew my whereabouts, how did he know I fed the homeless the third Saturday of every month?

I pulled into my parking space and noticed Tony's *Dodge* pickup truck wasn't there! Great! I'd have a minute or two to clear my master bedroom closet; the closet I'd promised Tony I would have cleared out last Tuesday.

I hurried up the steps to my condo. Just before closing the door who do I see pulling into the parking space next to my car? Tony!

The next hour was filled with Tony loading the materials in my house and measuring my closet. Happy Happy Joy Joy! Although Tony was only supposed to load my material and leave, he decided to spend a few minutes grouting the marble tile in the foyer that had been laid some 30 days earlier. He said it was ridiculous that I was still walking over and around the white tiles. I normally wouldn't have any work done on Saturdays, but I'd blown Tony off for a few weeks now, and he was becoming frustrated as he wanted to wrap up my rehab and move on to other more lucrative customers.

While Tony shot upstairs to complete the upstairs closet, his partner Nick began grouting and laying new tile in the foyer. Just as I was thinking today was a good day, I see Rick walk by my window. He impatiently rings the doorbell several times as if to say, "Hurry up and let me in." He had no key; he paid no rent, and he was no longer welcomed in my home.

I immediately shot to the door and vowed this would be the last time he stopped by unannounced or announced for that matter. I was prepared to offer up a few choice words. But first, I had to stretch my five-foot, two-inch frame over Nick who was laying tile directly in front of the door. Unable to reach the door knob, Nick intervened but was unable to unlock the door as he was twisting the latch in the wrong direction. Tony, who was watching this pitiful site from the kitchen, calmly walked over and used his six-foot, three-inch frame to lean over Nick and open the door.

Before I had a chance to light into Rick, he aggressively steps over Nick nearly kicking him in the head, sizes up Tony momentarily, and gives me the head nod as if to say, "Get upstairs right now." He marched up the 16 steps to my bedroom, with me hot on his trail.

First, Mr. Wright; now Tony and Nick. Rick had crossed the line invading my private space and subtly intimidating my contractors. It was on and cracking. The South Bronx in me was about to make a long overdue visit.

Rick slammed my bedroom door and immediately turned into a lamb. He apologized profusely about the insane calling; he told me he's sorry for barging in unannounced, but it was urgent we spoke, hashed things out, and got back together. He threw me off-guard with his meek and humble approach—then sheepishly slipped in questioning me about who the guys were downstairs. He became even more incensed when asking why there was a toddler in the house.

The uneasiness I was feeling around him reminded me of the controlling husband I was married to for nine and one-half years. Why had I listened to my girlfriends and tried to force this *relationship* to work? In hindsight, he displayed the controlling nature of my ex-husband. I made an awful mistake years ago, and I wasn't going down that ugly road again. I politely told him there would be no more dinners. No more phone calls. No more *us*!

I opened my bedroom door, and he sadly lowered his head, quietly walked down the stairs, and out of my life for good (or at least that's what I thought).

Two hours later Nick yelled that there was somebody at the front door. I excitedly exited my master bedroom closet hoping the visitor was my childhood girlfriend, Nicky. Nicky had promised to help me clear my closet. After five days of pleading with her, she'd finally showed up.

To my dismay as I began walking down the stairs to greet Nicky, I noticed Rick rushing up my staircase. He began all over again, in a rough and reckless manner, demanding to know who the kid was and why I had these strangers in my house.

He'd taken my kindness for weakness for the very last time. Day in and day out, I didn't have time to breathe, think, or complete school assignments.

Tony, who was carrying items from my master bedroom closet to my guest bedroom closet, heard the commotion. He hurried toward me and asked if everything was okay? Not getting the response he wanted, he clarified his question by asking, "Do we have a problem?"

The implication was clear to both Rick and I. If there was going to be a situation he was going to handle things on my behalf. While Rick was the size of an *NFL* linebacker, Tony had him by at least a few inches or so and could be a solid stand in for the Rock. Advantage Tony! I took this opportunity to tell Rick that he didn't pay any bills in my house, he wasn't my daddy, and his barging into my house was borderline criminal. I informed Rick that I was paying my crew by the hour and that he was cutting into their productivity.

There was no more sugarcoating things with Rick. I told him he had to leave and leave right then.

As Rick turned to leave, I began apologizing profusely to Tony and Nick. I'd never been more embarrassed in my life. Tony didn't deserve this craziness. He was only supposed to unload the truck. Now he's accused of being involved in some *Jerry Springer* mess.

Tony waved his hand indicating no apology was necessary and headed back into the master bedroom closet.

For the next hour or so, I focused on gathering the items for the new ministry I would start with Windy. I had boxes and boxes of new and barely used designer clothes, handbags, and shoes, many still with the price tags on them. These items would go a long way toward helping unemployed moms secure good paying jobs.

I headed downstairs to check on the guys, and before I knew it, I'd dosed off watching some kiddie show with Tony's son; or as my grandma would say, it was watching me. When I awoke two hours later, the place looked immaculate. The recessed lights in the kitchen had been installed, there was a beautiful *Moen* faucet in the kitchen, and my granite countertops had been laid perfectly. Portions of the interior had been painted and my California Closet was progressing nicely. My new house was beginning to feel like a home. To top things off, the condo had the amazing aroma of lavender. Fabulous. *Tony & Co.* had outdone themselves. To say I was excited would have been an understatement.

As Tony packed his tools, I headed to *Marcelo's*, a local Italian restaurant. I thought it'd be a nice gesture to get the guys a little chicken parmesan, and a garden salad topped off with a few pieces of garlic cheese bread. I was stopping by the ATM to grab cash for the guys, anyway. Sending them home with a decent meal was the least I could do considering they'd spent the past eight hours putting up with Rick's craziness and my empty fridge.

Besides, Tony's three-year-old son had been a real trooper the entire day, and I promised I'd get him a slice of authentic New York cheesecake as a treat.

As I waited in line at the ATM, I received a text from Tony saying Rick had returned, and he was pacing in the living room.

I immediately lost it. If it weren't for the two cars behind me in the drive-thru, I would have reversed right out of that stupid line. I couldn't get my money fast enough. I was livid, to say the least. I could feel my blood pressure and those two little frown marks that form over my brows when I'm really upset, rising as I sped to confront Rick.

As I peeled into my parking space, I nearly sideswiped Tony, who was standing next to his truck. I was driving like a maniac and for good reason. It was dark, rainy, and I was furious.

I was in such a rage that I left the door to my blue *Nissan* wide open. With my left hand, I slung the drinks and food at Tony. My right hand slapped the $1,500 in cash I'd just pulled from the ATM at him. I was passed my boiling point.

On this evening, there was no counting the money, getting a receipt for cash payment, or going over the agenda for the next day. Now that I think about it; I even left him with extra money.

No worries, I'd be back downstairs in a moment to apologize and settle up. But right now, I had bigger fish to fry.

As I raced up the concrete steps that led to my unit, I looked back at Tony, who said something about Rick not looking right. Did he mouth "Be careful"? I swiftly turned into my condo and nearly bumped into Nick, who was lugging a combination of trash and material out the front door.

Wide-eyed and frustrated, I scoured the kitchen, living room and downstairs bathroom looking for Rick. Fuming, I bolted up the stairs as if I was Jane Jetson wearing a power pack. With five steps to go, I realized he had turned out the lights and was watching television.

The nerve of him! I could imagine him kicked-backed with his shoes on my bed. He was in my room, my master bedroom. The final straw had been broken. I was stepping over the camel's back.

He had made the mistake of his life coming to my house for the third time unannounced. If he hadn't gotten the message the first two times, without question, he would now.

My left hand violently pushed the door wide open. I was going to lay him out good. He would be sorry he ever approached me nine and one-half months earlier. After being berated and undervalued in my tumultuous marriage of almost 10 years, I vowed I would never be anyone's pushover again. As my eyes adjusted to the darkness in my bedroom, I found myself staring face to face into the eyes of pure evil. I had never seen Rick so angry; he wasn't himself.

Everything I had bottled up; all of my frustration that I was going to fire off like a rocket launcher, dissipated. An unspeakable fear immediately struck me.

Rick's eyes were red with fury. They were glassy and pierced right through me. If looks could kill, I'd be dead. He was perspiring profusely, wet as if he had just stepped out of the shower.

Before I had a chance to yell or bolt downstairs, Rick blasted me with a vicious forearm to my temple. It felt as though I'd been hit by a crowbar! "God help me!" is all I could muster as I collapsed face down with his huge arms wrapped around my neck. I immediately knew I was in a life or death situation.

Flat on my back I began kicking and swinging like a wild woman. I reached for my phone to dial 911, but Rick caught my right arm and slammed the phone into the wall.

As he grabbed me by my hair and tossed me around the master bedroom, he began shouting, "Why did you lie? You're a liar! You're a liar!"

I was in the fight of my life. Where were my contractors? Couldn't they hear all the commotion? Exhausted after having the wind knocked out of me, I somehow managed to make it to the hall and stumbled to the staircase.

I thought, "Thank you, God!"

With Rick in pursuit, I grabbed the banister attempting to escape his clutches. As my foot touched down on the top step, Rick's out-stretched arm caught hold of my shirt and literally slung me back toward the hall.

One second I was heading toward safety, the next I was being spun and tossed into the guest bedroom like a rag doll. I landed face first with Rick's entire 260-pound body slamming on top of me. I was thrown with such brute force that it felt as though I shattered my jaw and every other bone in my face. The impact might have snapped my neck if Rick hadn't had me in a vicious choke hold.

This was no haphazard takedown. Rick knew exactly what he was doing. It was as if he practiced this move a thousand times. I landed with my arms under my belly and his knee on my back. I couldn't move. I couldn't breathe. How could I escape this dreadful wrath?

"No more. No more!"

I heard myself gurgle as I tried to steal one last gasp of air.

"Shut up and die, Denair! Just shut up and die!" Rick repeatedly screamed, "I'm not going back to jail! I can't go back to jail! You brought this on yourself! You didn't have to die tonight! This is all your fault! Are you happy now?"

He was hardened and deliberate. He was emotionless. He wasn't scared. His murdering me would be intentional. Rick choked me with such great fury that I knew it was only a matter of time before I'd be dead. I wasn't a quitter, but on this night, I'd given up hope of surviving this ordeal.

My 22-year-old daughter was in a toxic relationship. She had been pistol whipped and nearly thrown over a balcony while pregnant. If I died who would protect her?

In my mind, I saw the white chalk outline of my body.

I didn't curse God or say, "Why me?" My only regret was never telling my life story. I'd dreamed of inspiring millions. I'd survived almost 10 years of domestic violence, built a massive real estate empire, and interviewed childhood heroes Maya Angelo and Nikki Giovanni.

I'd cried my last tear. I was down to my last breath. Would I survive to see age 43?

Was my life really being snatched away by someone I'd known for fewer than 200 days?

2

Back to Life. Back to Reality.

I regained consciousness to blurred split vision.

It's as if someone had poured a pot of dry sand down my throat. Whatever I'd eaten the night before left a bitter dryness in my mouth. I was so thirsty.

Did I blackout?

I had no recollection of turning out the lights or climbing into bed. Everything was fuzzy. I had a splitting headache, unlike anything I knew before.

I thought, "Why is it taking me an eternity to clear my head and see clearly?" As things came into focus, I suddenly realized I wasn't in my bedroom lying comfortably in my California King bed. I was sprawled on the floor of my guest bedroom with my head pressed against the hardwood.

For the life of me, I couldn't understand why everything seemed so distorted. There was a profound silence in the room, but I sensed I was not alone.

As I struggled to turn my head slowly from left to right, I saw the vast reflection of Rick's frame through my mirrored closet doors. I hoped my mind was still playing tricks on me. I was taken aback to see Rick posted against the door fewer than six feet away from me.

I wanted to shout, "Rick, what are you doing here now?"

His eyes told me, "You better not open your mouth!" In the pit of my stomach, I knew something was terribly wrong. As I was trying to process Rick's eerie facial expression, my vague, faltering memory came racing back! Okay, the last thing I recalled was Rick choking me to death.

Oh God, Rick still had that murderous smirk on his face, but ironically he also looked bewildered and nervous. In my mind, I knew this nightmare wasn't over. I shouted to myself, "Denair, get up girl! Get away! Run!"

Something was wrong. My entire body was immobilized. I wanted to run, yell, and scream, but I couldn't move an inch. "Why am I pinned to the floor?"

While I was *back to life*, the *reality* was, the rest of my body hadn't regained its functionality. There was no feeling in my legs, arms, or torso. I badly wanted to hide my face in the floor to protect myself from whatever danger was looming to my exposed, vulnerable head. Unfortunately, I couldn't muster the strength to turn my face away from him. There would be no chance of me surviving part two of his onslaught once it began. I was completely and utterly helpless.

Every inch of my core wanted me to escape and live! The sad reality was I couldn't scream or blow a bubble if my life depended on it, and it did.

I was paralyzed with fear, but I was determined not to show it. God had spared me, brought me back to life, and I would survive whatever was about to happen. I could hear my guardian angel saying, "Get up, Denair! You will live and not die. Get up!"

Inexplicably, Rick lost it. Instead of pummeling me to death as I'd expected, he began pacing back and forth, violently slapping himself in the face. His actions were startling. He was mumbling profanities while tugging at his shirt. His eyes grew wider and more confused by the second.

> Three steps to the left, Slap. Slap. Slap. Three steps to the right! Slap. Slap. Slap.
>
> Three steps to the left, Slap. Slap. Slap. Three steps to the right! Slap. Slap. Slap.
>
> Three steps to the left, Slap. Slap. Slap. Three steps to the right! Slap. Slap. Slap.

Rick's internal battle easily went on for five minutes. I knew this movie, I saw it on *Lifetime*, but this time, it was my life, my story.

It was as if *life was imitating art far more than art imitating life.*

While Rick was focused on pummeling himself, I slowly began to regain the feeling in my arms, legs, and upper body. While keenly watching Rick's every move, I gingerly inched my body toward the bed, some three feet away. After making it to the bed undetected, I gently pulled myself off the floor, using the mattress as a crutch.

Once Rick noticed I was sitting on the bed, his eyes stalked me as if to say, "Where do you think you are going?" Although it certainly seemed like he was preparing his final assault, he never moved an inch toward me.

We were both on edge, neither of us took our eyes off the other, and no one spoke a single word. While I was ready to flee at a moment's notice, I knew we were both formulating a strategy and counter moves, once an initial strike was undertaken. From where I sat, it seemed as if there was no way out.

If I'd suddenly sprinted left, I clearly saw him cutting me off before I got to the door. If I were to bolt toward my right, in the direction of the window, I could see me making it safely to the window, but being hit with a devastating body blow before I had the opportunity to yell for help.

Unfortunately, I was in a no-win situation. The end game for me went from bad to worse. In my minds eye, I saw him finishing the job. I was boxed in, and Rick knew it.

As he slowly closed in on me, his eyes and clenched fists sparked intimidation, but I had to make a move and at least try.

Overpowering Rick physically seemed pretty unlikely, especially given my weakened condition. But mentally, that's where my advantage lie.

I silently prayed, "Guide my steps, oh Lord," and went after Rick. I extended my arms and calmly began caressing his murderous hands. I hit him with the kitchen sink next by saying, "Baby, please, let's stay together. I need you in my life."

I could tell he was staggering emotionally. He turned his face away as if to say, "Leave me alone, get back." In my mind, I said, "You're not getting off that easy, pal."

"Rick, Rick look at me," I gingerly stroked his face. "I love you unconditionally. I need you to believe in us. Boy, I love you more than you'll ever know."

Shocked and confused, Rick clenched his fists, and then violently shoved me clear across the room. He wanted me away; he wanted time to formulate his strategy.

In my heart of hearts, I knew he wouldn't hesitate to finish me off if I gave him time, so time was something I wouldn't give him.

I became the aggressor and immediately rushed him. There was no time to waste. He hadn't blasted me in the face with his fist, so I gave my strategy a 50/50 shot of working.

I had watched thousands of *Lifetime* movies. I knew if I were going to survive this nightmare I'd have to keep Rick calm and sell him on believing we would have a brighter, more promising future. I had to convince him of the role I played in all of this.

In addition to *Lifetime*, I also flashed back to how my mother convinced her would-be killer, the attacker who stabbed her over 60 times in her head, arms, back and chest, not to kill her. The composure Mom exhibited as her attacker wiped down the crime scene with bleach was stunning. She told him she'd forgiven him, offered to pray with him, and told him she wouldn't call the police or tell anyone.

If I yelled, screamed, or got excited there was no doubt in my mind Rick would quickly follow suit. I didn't scream, "I hated you!" or "You'll pay for this!" although I thought it. My only hope was acting my Mother Teresa role.

"How can I make this right, sweetie?" I said.

While I was intent on killing Rick with kindness, he was simply intent on killing me. As I reached out to touch his hands, he grabbed me by both wrists and shoved me away again.

His face was getting easier and easier to read. I saw him wrestling with what to do next. There was no keeping me away. I rushed back into the belly of the beast. I rubbed his chest and tried snuggling up against him. I whispered, "Rick, baby talk to me. If you left me, my life wouldn't, couldn't be the same. We have plenty of time to make this right. Don't we? Don't we?"

He looked down and away from me and then shoved me away. This time, I only flew back a few steps. My strategy was working (sort of). I wasn't out of the woods, quite yet. Between slapping himself in the head and slapping my hands away, he repeatedly shouted, "I'm not going back!" "I can't go back to jail!"

I had to convince Rick I was his *ride or die chick*! I had to make him believe we had an amazing future together.

> *Rick, this is a harmless, overblown mistake!*
>
> *Rick, I'm sad about what happened today.*
>
> *Rick, boy you know I love cooking for you. Can I make you something to eat?*

I was unrelenting. I was like Leila Ali, retired but undefeated, jab, jab, jab, jab. I had to keep Rick off-balance and wondering. Every time Rick knocked me down, I'd come rushing back. For me, this was a particularly dangerous game of cat and mouse, especially since Rick's rage was unsurpassed by anything I'd ever seen or imagined in my life.

For the previous 10 minutes, Rick tried with all his might to avoid looking directly into my eyes. I had to show him the softer side of Denair. I needed him to connect with me, rather than cut me. I had to convert his pain over the relationship into a passion for our future. I had to truly humble myself.

When Rick lowered his head to avoid contact, I practically kneeled in front of him so our eyes could meet. When Rick raised his head, I got on my tiptoes so he could see the compassion in my eyes (at least, that's what I wanted him to perceive). When he shifted left, I stepped to the left as well. For Rick, there was no escaping our *love* connection.

When I bent down, Rick could have easily kicked me in the face or blasted me with what I suspected was a gun in his waistband.

Despite my fears, I was trying to get closer to him. I kept telling myself, "Stay connected to Rick. Stay close." What other choice did I have? I wasn't going to die. I had work to do and lives to change. I know God kept me alive for this very reason. This was, without a doubt, my wake-up call.

Everything about Rick, from the bewildered look on his face to his constant slapping of his head, told me he was confused and searching for a way out.

Although Rick had me boxed in, in my guest bedroom, I was now the one applying the pressure.

I studied his tendencies. I had a good idea which words he'd be susceptible to and where his weaknesses were. Round IV!

> *Rick, look at me. You know I love you.*
>
> *Rick, this was a mistake that's entirely my fault. I should have spent more time with you; given you more attention. It was all me; I drove you to this!*
>
> *Rick, Rick, I'm tired of being alone. I'm ready for something real.*

Although I thought I was running mental circles around Rick, he still hadn't let me go. I brought out the big guns by telling Rick that whenever we were apart, I couldn't stop thinking about him.

I was no longer in front of him, but standing shoulder to shoulder with Rick, with my hand slightly on the doorknob.

I continued with a silent prayer. "Jesus, take the wheel, free me from this dungeon." After having my right hand painfully smacked off the doorknob several times, Rick no longer prevented me from touching the door. I gently inched the door open and quickly slid out of the room.

In my mind, I screamed "Thank you, Jesus! Thank you, Jesus!"

I raced down the 16 steps as if my feet were on fire, thinking, "Oh God, thank you for sparing my life. I'm free."

As I hit the bottom of the staircase, I was horrified to see my front door wide open. Was it open the entire evening? "Lord, why didn't anyone hear? Why didn't anyone help?"

As I slowed my stride to avoid slipping on wet marble tile in the foyer, Rick blitzed past me and slammed the down chute. My only thoughts were, "My God, save me! Please save me!"

Rick began spouting his rhetoric about not wanting to go back to jail. I didn't want Rick to over-think things. Now that I was downstairs, would my neighbors hear me I if yelled?

No! No! No!

I couldn't risk Rick becoming volatile again. Lord, how do I keep this disturbed individual off-balance and not focused on killing me?

Looking him in his eyes, I reassured Rick there was nothing to worry about. I promised I wouldn't tell a soul and that our relationship would be stronger than ever. "You'll see, wait until tomorrow. I have something really amazing planned for us." Despite my nerves, I spoke in a soothing, confident tone.

While I wasn't sure if he actually believed my story, I was absolutely certain he *wanted* it to be true.

With his face still looking twisted and confused. He exited my condo.

I immediately locked my door, gathered the pieces of my cell phone and bolted to my car. It had only been three minutes since Rick left; would he be outside my door or hiding in the parking lot?

It didn't matter. I couldn't be in that death trap of a house another second. I sped out of my subdivision like a menace. I had no preconceived destination. My only thought was to make sure Rick wasn't following me.

An hour later, I found myself standing in my brother's driveway. I had no recollection how I even made it there. It was only a 25-minute commute. Why had it taken so long? Where had I been? I didn't recall stopping at any red lights.

Tommy was somewhere in Europe, and I had his mini-mansion to myself. I crawled into the guest bedroom, wrapped myself in the blankets, and cried myself to sleep. Moments after I'd drifted off, my cell phone rang. Too sore and tired to look at the caller ID, I told myself it was either Tommy or mommy calling to check in on me. I hadn't spoken to either all day.

"Hello, Denair, what's up for tomorrow? What you got planned for tomorrow, Boo? You know I love you."

It was Rick, and I was livid! He'd beaten me, tried to strangle me to death, and then held me hostage for over two hours.

I shouted at the top of my lungs: "Why are you calling me, Rick? You tried to kill me! You are sick; really crazy! You tried to kill me, but you didn't. Now you're going to pay! Why would you think I would let you get away with this? You're going to jail! YOU ARE GOING TO JAIL!"

Nothing else Rick had to say was relevant. I simply powered off my phone. What was he thinking, calling me?

Moments later it hit me like a ton of bricks:

- *I'm home alone*
- *I boldly told Rick he was going back to prison*
- *No one in the world knew where I was*

What had I done? Before I hung up, was Rick trying to tell me he was outside Tommy's house? I was frightened beyond belief.

Rick now had an excuse to kill me. Once he caught me, I knew there would be no pardons or second chances given. I couldn't think straight. Had I turned on the alarm? Were all the doors and windows locked? I was fearful of leaving the room.

What had I done?

I found a screwdriver, turned off the lights, then slowly backed my way into the closet and waited!

3

Out of the Frying Pan. Into the Fire!

"You can't be brave if you've only had wonderful things happen to you."—Mary Tyler Moore

Kicking and screaming, I shouted, "Rick, don't shoot! Please don't shoot me!"

He simply laughed!

"Baby don't beg; it's not attractive. Did you think I wouldn't find you? Really!"

With the cold barrel of his gun pressed against my temple, Rick snatched me out of the closet by my hair and violently slapped me in my face.

"Didn't I tell you I wasn't going back to jail? Didn't I, Denair?" I thought, "How did Rick find me hiding in the closet? Why didn't I hear the alarm?"

As I saw the light flash from the muzzle of his gun, my last thoughts were, "Love shouldn't have to hurt."

"Wait! Why am I not dead? Why didn't the bullet hurt? This wasn't reality. It was a dream. This was only a dream!" I was a basket case. I'd been thinking about Rick catching and killing me all night long. My head was spinning. It was as if I was in the *Twilight Zone*. I didn't want to leave the safety of my closet. There was no good night's rest. I must have just dozed off. I was paranoid, I was exhausted, and I was hurting all over.

I powered on my phone and immediately received a call from Tony. He told me as I ran through the doors of my condo to confront Rick that he'd feared that would be the last time he saw me alive.

I cried... I cried... and I cried... "Why, why, why didn't you stop me, Tony?"

He said, "Denair, I tried to warn you, but you didn't listen. You didn't stop! You just dashed up the staircase. While you were at the store picking up takeout last night, your ex returned. Nick, and I were packing our gear and paid him little attention. Out of nowhere, he began talking real reckless and aggressive toward me. He asked me, did I know who he was? It was as if dude was interrogating me, Denair!"

"What is the nature of your business here? Whose son is that? Why is Denair watching him?"

"I immediately texted you to let you know he had returned. The heat was quickly rising in the living room. Dude didn't look normal. He was sweating, and he kept his head down shielding his intentions. I'm from the streets; I could tell something was about to jump off in a serious way. My son was sitting inches away from Rick and I was on the opposite side of my son. I moved little Ray Ray to my right, away from Rick. I prepared for the worst. I had an eight-inch sheetrock knife on my right hip. I positioned my hand to grab it if your boy so much as flinched.

"I gave Nick the *nod*, indicating he should go check who Rick had outside in the car waiting with him. Nick came back in and gave me the *all clear*.

"Your man either had to be carrying heat, or he was simply on something real bad that night. I decided to diffuse the situation by simply waiting outside.

"Rick invited me to stay. Ignoring him, I placed little Ray Ray in his car seat and waited to speak with you. Nick wanted to go back upstairs to handle the dude. If I hadn't had my son, I wouldn't have left. Little man had been at your place the past eight hours, and I needed to get him home.

"You jetted in the house so fast, without allowing me to get a word in. Although we had finished packing the truck, I waited outside to insure there wasn't a problem. Since I didn't hear any commotion, I assumed everything was okay. To be on the safe side, I called Tommy, multiple times, while circling your cul de sac. I thought about calling the police, but surmised at worst, you might be having a lovers quarrel. I didn't know what type of relationship you guys had. I didn't want to overstep my bounds. Maybe he was always this aggressive or just acting out because we were there? I simply didn't know.

"I easily called your cellphone 20 times over the next hour or so. I was relieved to finally reach you about 9:30 last night. You'd mentioned something about driving to your brother's house.

"I'm heading to *Home Depot* now to pick up some more paint. What time will you be home? I'd love to finish your closet by noon.

"Denair, Denair, Are you still there? What's up? Is everything okay? Speak up, I can't hear you!"

"Huh? What?" I whispered, with teardrops soaking my shirt. I quickly hung up the phone! I wanted to say something, but I couldn't. I was a mess and definitely still in shock, but I was angry with Tony and I was angry with Nick. Why didn't they say something? I was trying to make sense of it all, but I couldn't. I was so confused and mad at myself!

Why did he do that to me? He looked so scary; everything happened so fast. I can't wait to get him for this!

Was I still in danger? I didn't know what to do, think, or how to feel.

Should I call Tommy? I didn't even hear the phone ring, just "Dee, Dee. What's up? I'm getting ready to board," Tommy said in a rush. "What's wrong?" he repeated a few times.

"He tried to kill me," I finally mumbled. "What, I can't hear you? Speak louder, there's a lot of noise here." "Rick tried to kill me. He attacked me last night." Tommy said, "Rick. Rick. Your Rick? What happened, are you okay? Did you call the police? Where are you? Where is he now? Are you alone? What happened?" Tommy was going so fast I couldn't keep up. I faintly responded with one, "Yes."

Giving Tommy my cloudy details was a struggle. Tommy's voice was cracking as he insisted I quickly go to the sheriff's office where the incident occurred and report Rick's attempted murder and imprisonment. "Dee, go right now!" Just as I was hanging up, Tommy managed to squeeze in, "Don't go alone!"

I wish he were here. I desperately needed him, but he was a million miles away. Tommy's instructions were easier said than done. While the thought of leaving the house petrified me, I was more anxious about sharing this horrific story with the police. Would they believe me or try to blame this on me? I can hear them now, "Really, and then why didn't you come in last night or call 911?"

I had absolutely no faith in the police, especially after being carted off to jail over a decade ago. While the thought of Rick getting away with this was not an option, I had to find the courage to report what he did to me.

Although it had been 15 years since I was arrested for defending myself against my abusive ex-husband, the memory of being handcuffed in front of my screaming six and eight-year-old children was like an open wound that wouldn't heal.

The embarrassment and shame I carried for nine and one-half years, then being arrested the first time I called 911, was the driving force behind my fleeing the state of New York. I was so disgusted by the entire criminal justice process. I couldn't believe the callousness of the police officers that shoved me into their blue and white. They didn't even let me get dressed. They accosted me like I was a hardened felon as I pleaded, "There must be a mistake. I'm the one who called!" Hmmm, I'm supposed to trust the same officers who swore to protect and serve me? Just the thought of it nauseated me.

Was Rick conniving enough to possibly injure himself and claim I'd harmed him? Would he portray being the victim? I'd seen this movie up close and personal before, and it ended with me sharing a cold, urine-stenched cell with 50 ladies whom I'd rather not see again.

I screamed like crazy, and my stomach was in knots as I shivered at the thought of visiting the precinct alone. I called my cousin Veronica; she'd be my anchor.

As Veronica and I began the 30-minute trip to Crofton, Maryland, I suddenly realized I didn't know Rick's address. It wasn't in my cellphone or anywhere at Tommy's place. A few weeks back I'd faxed a number of documents to Rick's employer on his behalf. Maybe his address was still somewhere around the office. We were 15-minutes from the office, but I didn't want to waste time. I told Veronica I knew exactly how to get there, but I didn't know the name of the street or subdivision. I suggested we drive-by, snap a picture of the address, and keep it moving.

Despite all I'd been through the past 12 hours, I had a moment of clarity; or so I thought!

The fear of me walking into the precinct without his exact street address far outweighed my fear of him catching me in his neighborhood. I highly doubted the police would view me as credible if I couldn't furnish Rick's address. I told myself, "Girl, you will be fine." What were the chances of Rick being in front of his house at 7:30 in the morning, anyway?

As Veronica turned down Rick's street I was immediately paralyzed with fear. I shouted for Veronica to stop the car. "There's Rick!"

Staring at us fewer than 30 feet away was Rick! What had I gotten myself into? My God, had Rick spotted me? As Veronica pulled her hat down in an attempt to cover her face, I dove into the back of Veronica's van and buried myself under the bags of laundry and cleaning supplies. Did Rick know Veronica owned a dry cleaners? Had he ever seen her drive this van before?

Veronica began panicking! She couldn't reverse or stop on the tight two-lane street. We stood out like a sore thumb in Rick's remote community. For the life of me, I couldn't understand why we were driving at such a snail's pace. Would the light tint on the window prevent Rick from seeing inside? "Go, go, go!" Why didn't she just zoom past Rick?

Veronica turned her head and whispered, "It's okay, Denair, he didn't recognize me."

I was in straight panic mode. What Veronica didn't know was that

Rick lived in a cul de sac, and we'd be circling back by him 10 seconds later. On our return trip by Rick's place, Veronica stole a look at the mailbox and then sped out of the neighborhood.

Once we turned left off Rick's street and exited the community, Veronica gave me the *all clear* signal and waved me back into my seat. Unsettled, I focused my attention on the rear-view mirror. For the next 10-minutes, my heart beat at such a frenetic pace that I just knew it would rip through my shirt and explode! The fact that we'd just pulled into the parking lot of police headquarters didn't allow for a calming down period.

Although I should have felt safe, I told Veronica I was feeling very anxious and nervous. I didn't feel comfortable reliving the tumultuous events that occurred less than 12 hours earlier. I simply wanted to escape.

After a short prayer, Veronica held my hand and escorted me into what could only be described as a modern day Mayberry police precinct. While the sign above the door read, "To Protect and Serve," this was more like a ghost town, than a hub of law and order.

There were no phones ringing, no lawyers screaming about due process for their clients, or prisoners eyeballing me. No suspects were being shuffled back and forth from interrogation rooms or officials snapping mug shots. Chaos and confusion was not the order of the day.

I was seated in the lobby for all of 30 seconds before two officers warmly greeted me. They address me as "Ma'am" and guided me through the small, inactive precinct. They spoke to me in a calm and respectful manner. I was offered water, coffee, and soda, all before I began speaking. As I relayed the story of how Rick tried to kill me in a jealous rage, I was amazed at how I had the undivided attention of the only two officers in the station.

Officer Gomez kept telling me to relax and tried to reassure me that I was in a safe place. He expressed that my bloodshot eyes were evidence of asphyxiation. He went on to say that it is consistent with being strangled to death from lack of oxygen to my brain. Officer Gomez stated, "You're lucky to be alive." The tears just began to flow; first, down my left cheek and the second tear squeezed out from my right eye. And before I knew it, I was wiping my nose and my eyes in one clean sweep with the back of my hand. My lap was drenched as my head hung heavy on my neck. Someone handed me some tissues, but in my weakness, I still did not want to fall apart in front of them. I cleaned my face and blew my nose before raising my head. Veronica pulled her chair in closer to me and began rubbing my arm and back.

I was mentally, physically, and emotionally drained. As I continued speaking, out poured a broad range of emotions. I was talking fast and slow. Sometimes there was profound silence as I tried to recall all the details. As I heard myself telling the story, it sounded unbelievable. The events that took place seemed almost comical, even though this was a very intense and serious situation.

I'm sure I lost the officers a few times while describing what took place. Their facial expressions and body language encouraged me to continue as I sometimes took long pauses and held my head down in shame and embarrassment. This small, quaint precinct was a Godsend. My fear of being railroaded or arrested for making a complaint was fading. The officers frequently called me by name, took copious notes, and asked many follow-up questions. They seemed genuinely concerned, and I could tell they weren't going to sweep this under the rug.

I was so relieved, but I didn't want to get too excited, too soon. Rick was still on the streets!

The officers were highly surprised and offended that a crime of this nature had taken place in their backyard. They were even more shocked to learn Rick was sending me a series of threats, combined with love notes via text at the very moment they were taking my statement. The officers pulled their chairs in closer as they got more engaged and ultimately guided me on responses to send to Rick. They offered their sincere apologies and told me they'd handle the case with a sense of urgency.

I accepted their apologies but took their talk of moving on my case quickly with a grain of salt. I simply chalked it up to tough cop talk.

"Look, look, officer; here is a text from Rick, apologizing for hurting me and asking me to meet him at a hotel in Philadelphia." The next read, "Denair, you're mine for life. Let's turn this negative into a positive." The following text listed the hotel's address, along with his room number.

I threw my hands up. I could no longer subscribe to Rick's incredible foolishness. I slid my phone to the officers for their review and headed to the ladies room to regroup. Upon my return from the restroom, a forensic photographer greeted me. Surprisingly, she was the only person to enter the precinct in five hours.

Ms. Klean introduced herself to me and gave me her card. She explained that she would exit the room for a few minutes to give me time to undress. She said she needed to record any signs of the attack on my body. She also asked if the attack included a sexual assault as well. I answered, "No," in a very quiet voice and I could see that my reaction concerned Ms. Klean. The thought had never entered my mind that he could have raped me as well. He did have me pinned on the floor and overpowered me without hesitation. I responded again and said there was no sexual assault although the thought alone gave me chills. I just whispered to myself, "Thank you, Lord!"

As Ms. Klean reentered the room, she put on her gloves, pulled out her camera, and began thoroughly examining me in the middle of the room with only my underclothes. She asked me to recall the gory details again as she drew circles on my body, and her flash was blinding me. She was courteous, but straight to the point. Before Ms. Klean exited the room, she recommended that I go to the emergency room for a full checkup. She also stated that I would be extremely sore for a few days to a week and cautioned me that the bruising will be more evident by that evening or the next morning. "Please feel free to contact me if necessary and note anything that you think I've missed," she said, then she was gone.

After having the trauma to my neck, back, head and eyes documented, I was alerted with, "We *almost* caught him!" Unbeknownst to me, officer Gomez and his partner called in some favors to fellow officers in Philadelphia, Pennsylvania and asked them to apprehend Rick. They explained that Rick was a person of interest for attempted murder in Maryland.

The Philly officers called Rick's hotel and confirmed he was a registered guest. They followed up the call by quickly sending a number of patrol units to take him into custody. Within minutes, the hotel had been cordoned off and searched. Rick had escaped! The officers surmised Rick was tipped off by someone in the hotel's front office.

As I finally headed back to Tommy's house that evening, I was comforted by knowing these two strangers, especially officer Gomez, who had acted so swiftly and decisively on my behalf. There was no doubt they were genuinely vested in making sure justice was served.

While an incredible weight was lifted, the reality was that Rick was on the lam, and I wouldn't relinquish my fears completely until he was captured. Officer Gomez repeatedly emphasized that Rick was more dangerous than I suspected. He announced that he assigned a patrol car to Tommy's house, and they would canvas the neighborhood for any suspicious activity during the night.

As Veronica drove, I realized I was nervously bending a card in my hand. It was Officer Gomez's card with his cell phone number handwritten on the back. I vaguely recall his parting words as I dreaded what he had learned about Rick to make him go to such measures to ensure my safety.

Having my very own bodyguard was no easy feat, considering Tommy lived 25 miles and three police jurisdictions from officer

Gomez's precinct. I was confused but grateful that God sent an angel my way.

Reversal of Fortune

Monday began on a high note with me picking my mother up from the airport. She has always been my number one supporter. However, I quickly unraveled once I arrived at the precinct as instructed, for follow-up questioning. Officer Gomez introduced me to the two detectives who were assigned to my case.

When I was offered lukewarm greetings and so-so pleasantries, I sensed I was in for a daunting interrogation.

My efforts to share the details of my near-death experience were greeted with cold stares and callous attitudes. I was absolutely floored! How could this be? Fewer than 24 hours ago, I'd gotten the VIP treatment. I'm telling you, the more in-depth the story got as I shared, the more detective Morales's body language signaled she had checked out. She was completely cold, and she wanted me to know it. Her eyes said, "I'd seen my share of tears, and frankly, my dear, I'm not phased."

This initial meeting felt more like I was being treated as a hostile witness on the stand rather than an invitation to share my agonizing survival. After 30-minutes of her badgering, I wasn't shocked to hear her say she had spoken with Rick. She continued by saying he seemed like a pretty decent guy. "Ms. Huggins, could this all be some type of mix-up?

"Ms. Huggins, Rick indicated you guys were still actively dating and you weren't broken up.

"Ms. Huggins, Rick said you became agitated when he accused you of cheating with your contractor. He mentioned you yelled a bit, but things calmed down shortly thereafter.

"Ms. Huggins, Rick isn't on the run, but on a preplanned trip out of town to visit his family.

"Ms. Huggins, would you like to amend any portion of your statement from yesterday?"

Was I hearing her straight? I looked at my mom and the other detective in disbelief! The feeling of being brutally attacked came rushing back. It was as if she had pushed Rick out the way and commenced choking me herself. I was sick to my stomach but wanted to poise myself before I responded. I could feel the anxiety welling up and felt like the room was closing in on me.

I knew there would be no manhunt for Rick. I'd be on my own. I wanted to run out of there and give her a piece of my mind, but I knew that would not help. I simply responded by pointing to my neck, where the strangulation marks were still visible and said, "I guess I choked myself as well?"

I needed to hide, but I couldn't. I had a meeting with the state prosecutor.

Indeed, I'd find a warmer audience. It couldn't get any worse, could it?

While I waited in the hall of the courthouse, I contemplated slipping out through the side door and making this trip another day. Just as I turned to leave, a young African American lady with a gracious smile approached me, extended her hand, and announced she'd be working on the case.

I thought things couldn't be more perfect.

Here I am fretting about the treatment by the lead detective; now God sends me an attorney who looks like she could be my first cousin or college classmate. I quietly whispered to Mom, "Won't God fix it?"

Relieved that some old misguided man would not be (mis)handling the case, I was caught off-guard when my new *shero* began peppering me with a series of twisted questions. I couldn't believe how she was coming at me. There was no hint of sympathy or comfort. Her warm smile had long faded. I wanted out of this whirlwind and wished there was some way for me to march out of her office and press the reset button. Does she recognize that I am the victim and not the accused? I'm here to help the state put away a hardened criminal. Or did she have another objective?

"Ms. Huggins, why did you wait 10 hours to report the alleged crime? What are you not telling me?

"Ms. Huggins, on the night in question, why did you have other men working in your home in the first place?

"Ms. Huggins, what did you do to initiate this alleged attack? Something is not adding up."

Was the Prosecutor prosecuting me? Was she clear on her role, to seek justice? I didn't deserve to be re-victimized. I understand that she was not there to hold my hand, but she could save the harsh tone and deep stares for the "alleged attacker."

This is why victims are afraid to come forward. They fear the harsh and unpleasant cynicism that fills the halls of justice.

I was quite familiar with legal procedures and had implemented many tactics while screening and preparing witnesses for trial. However, over the last five years, I had not utilized any of these strategies to win a case.

As a matter of fact, I had a degree in criminal justice and was only six credit hours from completing another. I was already looking into law schools. I believed that the criminal justice world could use a Denair to stand up for those that could not stand up for themselves. As a certified domestic violence counselor, I was proud that our firm did more *loving* than lawyering. At that moment, I was expecting an impartial voice rather than a judge and jury.

It took everything inside me to keep from jumping on the conference table and start yelling, "Hello! I'm the victim here!" I could only classify my first meeting with the prosecutor as a colossal failure. As I left her office, I had a profound sense of emptiness.

Nothing that took place on this day left me with the confidence that she would be prosecuting Rick to the fullest extent of the law. On the contrary, I was concerned that the prosecutor wouldn't even charge Rick. I felt so broken, and I knew this was only the beginning. He'd already won over the lead detectives over the phone, now his smoke and mirrors act was casting a fog of doubt of even going forward.

Rick's attack on me was unprovoked, malicious, and intentional. Where was the outpouring of support for me within the legal system? Would the prosecutor be more comfortable with my body on a slab before she agreed to pursue this violent felon?

I began the day very confident that law enforcement was 100% on board in its pursuit of Rick. By the end of the day, I just didn't know. Why would I make up these stories? Can't they see he is a master manipulator? I'd experienced Rick's wrath, and I knew he had the potential to kill if he hadn't already.

I wasn't married to Rick, but somehow he subscribed to the philosophy of "Til death do us part." I adopted two simpler ones, "Live to see another day," and "It's always too soon to quit!" —Norman Vincent Peale.

As I sat on the corner of my bed trying not to cry, I decided I'd become my own victim's rights advocate. Despite what officials thought, I believed I was in clear and present danger! Rick's threat wasn't just rhetoric to me. I'd regularly worked 12-hour days on legal battles for others. I told myself I'd work day and night until Rick was behind bars. I would get them all the proof and evidence they needed until they decided to pursue Rick rigorously.

At the crack of dawn, although I was suffering from extreme anxiety attacks all night and only slept a few winks. Between waking up in cold sweats, I slipped out of the house, bolted to my car and headed to the law office, which was only a few blocks away. Stepping out of the house alone was enough to make me lose my mind, but I had to push through my fears and put on my *big girl panties*. It was time to face the facts: I'd missed something huge in the first background check I ran on Rick, before initially agreeing to meet him for lunch.

I'd only run a quick, unofficial check nine months ago. That only pulled up a housing situation that he explained. So what was Rick hiding? What was behind his ranting about not going back jail? Did he just fabricate it Saturday evening to intimidate me? Geez, I was turning into a Nancy Grace. This time, I would plug Rick's date of birth and prior addresses into the firm's nationwide database. I was determined to catch up with Rick's criminal history before he somehow caught up with me.

I was on pins and needles as I waited for something to pop up on my computer screen. I was so uneasy that I panicked every time I heard a car alarm set or door slam. I had to get it together. I didn't want to stay in the office alone, but I didn't want to walk in the hallway or outside alone either. As I tried to stay focused, my mind kept drifting over all the things that made me uneasy about Rick.

For months, I had a strange feeling Rick was driving by the office just to ensure I was where I'd said I would be. What if he came searching this morning? The thought of Rick was driving me insane. I began to second-guess myself and wondered if I was overreacting.

I was beating myself up, disgusted as to why I gave Rick another chance after he'd shown his controlling nature the night I attended the *Naturally 7* concert in Rockville, Maryland. Roger and Warren, the founders of *Naturally 7*, had been like brothers to me for nearly 30 years, especially as kids. We'd eaten at each other's houses, gone to church together, run track, and hung out all around the city. I was thrilled they'd become one of the top musical acts in the world. I'd seen them on *The Tonight Show with Jay Leno*, *The Ellen DeGeneres Show*, and *The Today Show with Michael Bublé*. Their a cappella tribute to Herbie Hancock at *The BET Honors Awards Show* was legendary. I hadn't seen my brothers perform live since we were in the choir together as teenagers. So when Roger called and said he had an extra ticket, I was all in.

Excited, I called Rick and told him the good news. He was flat, but that was beginning to be his norm. He started saying I never made time to go out with him. I ultimately invited him to come although I was only allocated one ticket. A few phone calls did the trick, and my very good friend would be allowed a courtesy seat, compliments of Roger. Rick declined under the pretense that he was not initially invited, so I went without him. I walked into the concert, powered off my cell phone and had the time of my life. After the show, a group of us took pictures, grabbed something to eat at the arena while we caught up, then I headed home.

Exhausted, I fell out cold on the bed and was still partially clothed. I was expected in the office earlier than normal the next morning to prepare for a key client later that day. Comatose, I was awakened by an ungodly banging on my door. Was someone trying to notify me of a fire? Eyes still closed, I stumbled to the door. It was none other than Rick. He asked why I hadn't picked up my cell phone while simultaneously darting by me toward my bedroom. As I headed into the hall restroom, I threw water on my face. I caught my bearings and realized what was going on. I was livid. Outraged, I stormed into my bedroom to tell Rick off. He wasn't in my bedroom, the living room, or kitchen. He was gone.

At that time, I was living in a 20-story condominium. It offered multiple layers of security. How did he get past the lobby? Had Rick been stalking me? I was fuming. I vowed never to speak with him again. Three weeks later I acquiesced and allowed him to meet me at the office for lunch. That was just 90 days ago. We'd only gone out four or five times since then. Why hadn't I stuck to my guns? Why did I listen to my girlfriends and give him another chance?

Why? Why?

As I turned my attention back to the computer screen, I was astonished to see there were pages and pages of information on Rick. I'd known Rick for nine months, but I really never *knew* him. I was fanning off a hot flash as my anxiety increased. I quickly slid out through the side entrance of our office, avoided the elevators, and ran down the back staircase to my car. I couldn't wait to show officer Gomez and everyone else what I'd learned about Rick!

As I sped to the Crofton Police headquarters, I felt so stupid for missing this. I could hardly keep my eyes on the road because I kept looking around and checking my rear-view mirror. Rick was a stone cold criminal and now that I had what I was looking for, I was even more afraid.

Rick wasn't the one for me, and I knew it from the start! I settled like so many other women. I had options, really good options. But I gave in to *Mr. Okay*, and now I'm paying the price.

I gathered my dossier on Rick, walked into the precinct, head held high, and asked to see detective Martinez. I was told she wasn't available. Without hesitation, I requested officer Gomez.

Officer Gomez appeared genuinely excited to see me. When we arrived at his desk, it looked as if he'd been expecting me. There were stacks of articles, documents, and files, all about Rick on his desk. "What a coincidence," I said. "I have a file on Rick too."

I couldn't believe what I was reading. His dirty little secrets were more frightening and preposterous than I'd ever imagined. The string of dropped charges and horrific stories were jumping off the pages at me in living color.

- Kidnapping his ex-wife in broad daylight from a gas station with an accomplice! Throwing her in a car and tying her up. If not for her being able to miraculously access her cell phone, she might be six feet under today. Case closed! Charges dropped!
- Fleeing an armed state trooper who was attempting to pull him over because his license plate indicated he had an outstanding warrant. After a lengthy high-speed chase, Rick exited the vehicle and body-slammed the armed trooper. Case closed! Charges dropped due to a technicality!
- Multiple accounts of domestic violence by an ex-girlfriend who eventually declined to follow through and press charges. Case closed! Charges dropped!

As I sat with officer Gomez, I began to shake uncontrollably. Rick was a fearless monster who acted on impulse, without regard for his life or anyone else's.

Attacking an armed state trooper? Kidnapping with an accomplice in broad daylight? Did Rick have any limits? There was no telling what other skeletons Rick had in his closet!

Officer Gomez leaned forward with an uneasy look on his face and confided there were other questionable things in Rick's file; unconfirmed rumors, that, if true, made Rick and his associates a very, very dangerous group affiliated with underworld ties—the Mob!

When officer Gomez mentioned the "underworld," my mind immediately raced back to a frantic call I received regarding my 21-year-old daughter. The vicious incident involved dragging, kicking, punching—nothing good. I feared for my daughter's life as well as my grandbaby's life.

I pulled my car over, trying to process what I'd just heard. I needed to know whether Denika was currently safe. Why didn't anyone help? As I tried to make sense of what I was hearing, Rick, who was sitting in the car, calmly chimed in with "I'll handle him. Where does he live?" I reasoned Rick was just talking tough? What could Rick do? He was in the passenger seat of my car in Maryland while Denika and Lovie were somewhere in Atlanta. I was about to explode. I wanted to comfort and protect my daughter and her baby.

As I was making calls to rally the family there, Rick picked up his phone and placed a call as well. "Who do we have in the ATL to put in work?" Hearing only bits and pieces, his last words were. "Tomorrow. I need it done by tomorrow." There's no telling if Rick even had anyone on the other end. I thought he was simply puffing up his chest and talking tough. I shook my head, indicating to Rick, "Whatever you just did, I need you to undo." Eight hours later Rick was still all worked up at the thought of a man putting his hands on my daughter. It's like he'd blown a gasket. He wanted to take action. He wanted the guy *touched*!

In hindsight, after listening to officer Gomez, it was likely Rick was putting out a hit from Maryland!

Officer Gomez insinuated that my life in Maryland might never be the same. He kept saying this is a bad guy. He was convinced that Rick was a ruthless individual who would likely seek me out and try to silence me. He let me know it was imperative I stayed vigilant. In my mind, I told myself, there's no telling whom Rick's connected to or what he's capable of!

Although officer Gomez was being polite, he wanted to know how a nice church girl got involved with this thug. He urged me to pay attention to signs more closely and always follow my gut. I was still in the same clothes since the attack and had not been back home.

Officer Gomez arranged for another cruiser to meet him as he escorted me to my house to grab a suitcase full of clothes. He suggested that I stay someplace safe until Rick was apprehended and encouraged me to take everything I needed.

True to his word, as I arrived at my condo for the first time since the incident I was comforted by seeing one of officer Gomez's patrol units waiting in my assigned parking space. This gesture let me know they were putting a great deal of credence to my complaint. It also let me know they believed there was an elevated threat on my life.

After packing a few bags of clothes and other essentials, I was led out of the subdivision by my security detail and sent on my way. Concerned about being followed, I zigzagged all the way to Tommy's house without signaling as I pulled onto his street.

Throughout that evening, I received calls from many different officers. Their messages were surprisingly the same: "We're here if you need us." They each offered their private numbers and insisted that I bypass 911 in the event of an emergency since they would mostly likely be in the vicinity.

It was as if the entire force was focused on my protection, except for Morales, the primary detective assigned to the case. The abundance of concern was spearheaded by none other than officer Gomez.

Three hours after resting my head for the evening, I received a call from a blocked number. Was it Rick again? He had been blowing up my phone all day with calls and texts! Deep down inside I couldn't take anymore. I wanted him to stop. I needed him caught. I wanted to break down and cry.

As I picked up, I heard a familiar voice. "Good evening, Ms. Huggins. This is officer Gomez. Were you sleeping?"

I wanted to say, "It's 3:30 in the morning.

"Thank you for checking in on me again," I said. To know the officers were driving miles out of their way and calling me when they were off-duty was unheard of. Officer Gomez continued! "I have some fantastic news. You can sleep well the rest of the evening. Rick was arrested 30-minutes ago in New Jersey."

"When? How?" I had a million questions rushing through my head, all at once. I could feel the blood coursing through my veins. I was overwhelmed with joy and uncertainty. I didn't know if I'd be required to show up in court in the morning to pick Rick out of a lineup or whether I had to go to the precinct immediately to ID him.

He told me he didn't have the particulars yet, but he believed Rick was being held in a detention center three hours away. Because Rick was captured in another state, he anticipated it taking anywhere between five days and five weeks to have Rick extradited to Maryland to face charges. Officer Gomez concluded the call by saying, "It'll be a long day tomorrow so try and get some rest."

I jumped up in excitement and stumbled over the furniture. For the past few days, I had hunkered down behind one of the large Italian sofas in Tommy's living room. It was kind of my fort. Anyway, concerned about my sudden eruption, Mommy yelled, "Is everything okay? Do I need to call 911?" Although my mom was a long skirt wearing, Bible believing Christian, she was no punk.

Immediately, my mind went to one of my favorite scriptures I learned as a child:

"But they that wait upon the LORD shall renew their strength; They shall mount up with wings as eagles; They shall run, and not be weary; And they shall walk, and not faint." (Isaiah 40:31).

I was walking on eggshells. It had been nearly eight hours since officer Gomez called and told me about Rick being captured. What was going on? Was there a hiccup in the arrest? Had New Jersey released Rick irrespective of Maryland's warrant on attempted murder charges? Did they even have the right person in custody? I was coming unglued.

I'd called detective Morales, the state prosecutor, and my recently assigned victim's advocate, all to no avail. I didn't know how much I could take. I was rapidly losing faith. I finally called officer Gomez, although he was off-duty. He apologized profusely for detective Morales not communicating the details of Rick's arrest. Ten minutes later, officer Gomez called me back and told me if I wanted an unofficial update, to simply Google Rick's full name.

In moments, I powered up my Mac and typed Rick's full government name into my search bar. Bam! Four seconds later I was staring at Rick's mug shot and 20 articles related to how an intoxicated fugitive on a bender crashed into a government building.

Rick's wellbeing was not at the top of my list. I couldn't care less. I just was concerned that he was wearing shiny, lockable bracelets.

My initial thoughts were, "Who gets liquored-up and crashes into a building staffed by emergency service personnel when they're on the run?" My only hope was that Rick didn't manipulate New

Jersey officials into releasing him before Maryland sent the paddy wagon to pick him up.

Rick had dodged the police for 36 hours. I was so grateful he was in custody. As I read and reread the articles, I was floored by the irony of how he was caught. I sarcastically told Mom, "You can't make this stuff up!"

Although it wasn't as bad as a story Mom and I shared that involved some guys who robbed a video store, then inadvertently dialed 911 after sitting on their cellphone in their rear pocket, it was pretty close.

There was no high-speed chase. He wasn't cornered after a deadly shoot-out with authorities. No! Rick, the person who wanted me dead a few days earlier, was literally caught asleep at the wheel. Per the officers who apprehended him, Rick was found sleeping, blocking the driveway of a local firehouse! The article continued, saying there was extensive damage to his vehicle as well.

Upon waking Rick, the officer noticed he reeked of alcohol. Once Rick's tag was run, he was identified as a dangerous fugitive. He was placed under arrest after failing a field sobriety test. En route to the jail, officers were updated on Rick's slew of charges against me which included: second-degree attempted murder, first and second-degree assault, false imprisonment, and reckless endangerment.

Highlighted in the middle of the page it stated, "We were certainly happy we were able to grab this guy from Maryland and take a dangerous guy off the street," said Hopewell Police Chief, George Meyer."

As my mom and I read several other related articles, I told her if this weren't the imbecile that tried to choke the life out of me, I'd probably be in stitches laughing at this. If Rick had his way, I'd be in a morgue and my family would be writing my obituary rather than reading the good news of his arrest across the Internet.

Although he was captured, I wasn't completely out of the woods yet!

Did I err in thinking I 'd be an indispensable part of the prosecutor's case? Word of Rick's arrest was headline news on local TV channels, made the front page in several newspapers, and started going viral on the Internet. However, the prosecutor hadn't seen fit to personally reach out to me. I was stunned!

Would the disengaged prosecutor be willing to convince Governor Martin O'Malley's office that allocating the money and manpower to return Rick to Maryland was a proper use of the taxpayers' money?

I was on edge awaiting word on Rick's possible extradition to Maryland. The delay was particularly troubling after learning nearby cities, like Philadelphia, didn't pursue 90% of the violent felony suspects who fled their jurisdiction to avoid prosecution.

After speaking with officer Gomez, my fears were allayed. He unequivocally assured me there was a compelling reason for the state to incur the transportation cost associated, even though the state was on a tight budget. I relaxed a bit knowing Rick was one accused felon who wouldn't disappear in the wind. Officer Gomez went so far as to offer to personally drive to New Jersey to secure Rick's transport into the Maryland jurisdiction.

What? Best cop ever!

Now that I knew Rick was secure in his six-by-eight suite in an exclusive gated community (aka cell), I hoped my life would slowly regain normalcy until the trial.

I thought heading to the office for a while might be a good idea. To my dismay, the practice was as discombobulated as my personal life. There were dozens of calls to return, foreclosure documents stacked from floor to ceiling, and a string of errands to run.

I closed the door, rolled up my sleeves, and began clearing my desk. I wasn't in the mood to chat it up with the staff or do any consultations. Nor was I looking for a pity party or a pat on the back. I only wanted a little peace and to get some work done. I was so overwhelmed the past few days I hadn't even told all my siblings about the attack yet.

My mind was racing. I knew it was time to take a break when I looked down and saw I'd been shuffling the same three files on my desk for nearly an hour.

I was trying my best to behave normally. Everyone was always used to me being the burden bearer, wearing an S on my chest. I needed to decompress. Maybe I'd call my big brother and tell him what happened to me. We'd been as close as any brother and sister could be. He was the one who taught me how to tie my shoes. While I could have chosen to attend any high school in New York,

I selected his school to be near him. When it was time for college, I enrolled in a school 1,000 miles away to be by his side.

Deep down, I didn't want to share the story. The wounds of the attack were scorching my insides. I just wanted the pain, the embarrassment, and the humiliation to go away. I didn't want to keep reliving the details of how Rick nearly choked me to death.

Completely in a fog about how I was going to tell my brother, Eddie, I hadn't noticed my assistant standing over me. She told me there was an urgent call holding for me. "Was it the prosecutor finally checking in?" I wondered.

The voice on the line said, "Hello, Denair! How are you? I'm checking in to see how you're doing?"

Startled, I answered, "Fine, thank you." I didn't recognize the voice. I told myself, I'd only told a few people. This is exactly what I'd feared!

The pleasant voice on the other end continued saying, "I'm not sure if you remember me; my name is Stacy. I met you a few months back at my all-white party. You came with Rick."

I adjusted my tone, indicating the disdain that was mounting. I abandoned my professional voice and got straight to the point. "What is the nature of your call?" I demanded.

I couldn't believe she had the audacity to tell me Rick was holding on the other line and that he wanted us to all get on the line together and figure out how to make this *thing* go away.

I was livid. "You're now a part of this investigation. Don't ever call me again!" I shouted.

Click! She got the dial tone.

He wanted this *thing* to go away? I wanted *Rick* to go away for a long time. I went from fuming at my desk to pacing back and forth in my office. She'd crossed the line. There was a restraining order against Rick, preventing him from calling or contacting me in any form.

I immediately left a message for the district attorney. Yes, it was only a brief call, but it just didn't sit well with me. I simply didn't know what Stacy was capable of. Stacy and Rick had been thick as thieves for years. She must be his sidekick. She'd even hired Rick as a counselor at her group home for troubled youth!

While waiting to hear back from the prosecutor's office, I was bombarded by calls. Still thrown off after the first call, I grew more uptight 10-minutes later when I received a call from a Dr. Jackson on my cell phone.

"Hello, Denair, I hope your day is going well. This is Dr. Jackson. I heard a lot of beautiful things about you." I'm saying to myself, "Dr. Jackson, who?" I didn't have any idea who Dr. Jackson was. Was she with the DA's office or victim services?

She continued in a very friendly, comforting voice. "I understand there was an incident between you and Rick. If there is anything I can do for you, don't hesitate to reach out to me. I've been where you are right now, and the important thing is not to overreact. Rick has a few kids. Please consider what might be in the best interest of everybody before you continue with these so-called charges. I've spoken to Rick, and he is remorseful. He'd like to talk directly with you and clear all of this up."

As Dr. Jackson continued lobbying on Rick's behalf, it hit me: Dr. Jackson wasn't just any ol' doctor. She was Rick's baby mama, the chick who was still crazy about him. She wasn't representing Victim Services. No! She was calling on behalf of Rick. What kind of game was she playing? She was one of the ladies who'd declined to press assault charges on Rick multiple times. I read about several of her chilling beatings at the hands of Rick in the police reports. I felt sorry for her. This was one therapist who was severely damaged herself.

Nevertheless, I was tired of her dilly-dallying. She'd already told the district attorney; Rick was a model father and all-around good guy.

"Let me be crystal clear, Dr. Jackson! I'm not sure what type of mind games you're playing. Rick tried to kill me, and maybe you like that rough stuff but you can explain this to the detectives. You are now officially part of the investigation too. Really, girl? Do not call me again!" I could still hear her pleading, "...But Denair, Denair!" as I slammed the phone down.

Conspicuously, just minutes after hanging up with Dr. Jackson, there was a call from Rick's cousin, an attorney. She only said, "I heard about what happened. I wish you the best."

I had a feeling Rick would be reaching out to other associates if his initial strategy to get me to drop the charges wasn't successful.

Being in jail wasn't a deterrent from Rick calling and harassing me. His ex-girlfriend, his employer, everybody and their mama was blowing up my cell. My thoughts were, "Who's next?" It did not matter; I would never drop the charges!

Given Rick's extensive history of violence against women, there was no way they seriously bought into his story. Is it just officer Gomez and I that can see him for who he really is?

Reluctantly, I decided to call *T-Mobile* and change my number. I had that number for almost eight years, but I had to cut Rick off at the pass and let him know his little stunt didn't work. My voice-mail was full, and I thought I should retrieve the messages just in case I missed any business calls over the last few days.

Every other message started off with, "Collect call from..." then Rick's voice would squeeze in a few cut-off words.

Denair, I'm sorry.

Denair, you're making a mistake!

Denair, I'm so in love with you.

Denair, I can't go back to jail.

Denair, don't take me from my kids.

Was Rick in jail or was he a telemarketer? Who was monitoring him? How in the world was he able to make so many calls from jail, to me, his alleged victim?

I was rattled, but I wasn't going to fold. Rick was not going to get off this easy. I asked myself what type of victim's advocate was I if I allowed this monster back out on the streets?

If he was willing to kidnap his ex-wife in broad daylight, at a highly visible gas station, what would he do to me? I had to stand my ground or die trying.

Two days after changing my cell number to avoid further harassment, I received a letter without the specific sender contact information. The address was a P.O. box in Trenton, New Jersey. As I unfolded the two pages, I scanned to the end and see, "Love, Rick."

This guy must really think he has game. I didn't want to entertain his jailhouse rhetoric! I immediately raced to the stove to torch that foolishness. Just as the flame reached the corner of the letter, I was like "What am I doing?"

Maybe the letter contained a confession that could be used by the prosecutors to put Rick away. My eyes shifted from left to right as I sighed and sucked my teeth. It read:

> *Dear Denair,*
>
> *First, let me start by saying I'm so apologetic to you and your family. I was afraid of being without you. I lost myself. I should have trusted you more or walked away. I know you can never forgive me, but I hope you remain who you are; gracious, beautiful, and very loyal to family and friends. I am waiting to be transported from Mercer County Jail back to MD to make bail. I apologize for letting my family and you down. You deserve a real man now, not a kid, a man who can control himself.*

I'm lying in my bunk thinking about all the fun we shared and the friend I lost. You made me a better person. Your smile made me feel warm inside. Losing my job made me pity myself and drive you crazy. I felt inferior to you because your job is on the fast–track and I'm still lost at 38.

I wish for you to find someone who treasures you and your kind heart. Never change who you are. You are an angel who tries to help everyone. I didn't appreciate it, so God will bless you with someone who does. My heart is so heavy without you. But good news! When I get back to MD, I am going to AA and anger management classes! Tell your granddaughter *I love her, ask your mom to forgive me, and tell your kids I'm sorry too. You can live your life. Please don't fear me! I will never bother you again, other than to give you my forwarding P.O. box. So this is the hard part, the goodbye hugs. I will always love you and never forget what we had. You are my best friend. Please forgive me and be happy in your life.*

P.S. Please live your life without fear of me. I will never harm YOU!

All I could think was, "Good; more evidence! Whatever to everything else, blah blah blah! Tell it to the judge."

Just five days after strangling me to death, he was a transformed man, and I'd miraculously become the best thing since sliced bread? I wasn't buying this for one second.

I summoned my inner Steve Harvey and dissected the letter as if it was a Strawberry Letter on his show. The more I read it, the easier it was to decipher Rick's true intent of the letter.

There was no need to read between the lines; everything was spelled out in black and white on the final line:

> *P.S. Please live your life without fear of me. I will never harm YOU!*

From what I read in his files, harming women was his specialty. So this letter was code for, "I WILL harm you."

For five days, he'd proclaimed to the police, the prosecutor's office, and his loved ones, that I made the entire tear-jerking story up and overreacted.

Was this a confession, threat, or both? Confessing he would hurt me; yeah, I got the message loud and clear.

If he hadn't harmed me in the first place, why was he saying I shouldn't fear him? Why the need for anger management?

What type of jail lets fugitives send outgoing mail, and threatening ones at that?

Rick's daunting words echoed in my head. "I TOLD YOU I WASN'T GOING BACK TO JAIL!" And he sealed it with a stamp that said, "FEAR ME!"

As I wrapped myself up tight in a blanket and curled up behind my couch fort, I whispered as the tears began to fall, "I'm not going to let you scare me. You will not win! You tricked me once, shame on me. Next time, shame on YOU! I see you now."

P.S. I won't harm you... P.S. I won't harm you...

I couldn't ignore Rick's threat on my life, especially since I'd already experienced his wrath!

Bail? Bail? Why? How?

Would the judge actually consider setting bail? What is going on? Did they forget Rick had $30,000 in cash on him when he was found sleeping behind the wheel of his car in Jersey, or that he fled the state?

A million questions flooded my mind.

What legit businessman carries that much cash in the trunk of his car? Whatever happened to travelers' checks or credit cards? As I listened to the voice on the other end, my mind began to drift. I was trying to get a word in, but they had an answer for everything.

I'd never seen Rick loaded with cash before. He'd been on workers' compensation from his construction job for nearly nine months and was always crying broke. Where did that money come from? My thoughts raced to officer Gomez's comments about Rick's associates.

Red flags and alarm bells immediately went off in my head. I put two and two together and quickly rationalized that money might be used to silence me! Although the police were keeping an eye on me like a hawk, in my heart of hearts, I knew it wasn't a matter of if, but when, Rick would come after me.

Fewer than 24 hours after reading Rick's jailhouse *love letter*, all of my worldly possessions were packed into a 26-foot *U-Haul* truck. I had called my son, who was away in college, my brothers, cousins, friends, and my mom to assist with the unplanned move, and I was out of there.

Everyone tried to discourage me from leaving town, especially the detectives and DA's office. They said, "Not to worry it was just a formality. He will never make bail."

Just 48 hours after I fled, I wasn't surprised to learn Rick had posted a $300,000 cash bond and was shackle-free whistling *Dixie* throughout Maryland.

What caught me off-guard was a frantic 10 a.m. call from my office assistant, Shequita, the very next morning after Rick's 11:45 p.m. release.

When she whispered, "He's here, Rick is outside right now," a massive shiver hit the center my spine! I instantly broke out in a cold sweat!

I could hear the terror in her voice. We were both paralyzed with fear! The only difference, Rick was fewer than 35 feet away from her! I shouted, Hang up and call 911!"

I was guilt-stricken for asking her to show the unit to a prospective tenant. I'd expected Rick to come after me. I didn't imagine he'd slip by the armed police officers guarding the entrance and exit of my subdivision!

"Denair, he hasn't gotten out of the car yet. He's circling your condo, leaning out the passenger-side of a white van I've never seen before. Okay, he is leaning back in the van, now he is looking all around as if he is clearly searching for your car."

Shequita went silent for nearly 15 seconds. It was like time stopped.

"Shequita, are you there? Are you okay? Are the officers still in front of the complex?"

"Yes, but I'm too scared to go outside. Rick knows me. I'm afraid! I'm so afraid I can't think right now."

I was hysterical, and I was hundreds of miles away. I could only imagine the fear that was piercing Shequita. I wanted to tell her it'd be okay, but I would have been lying. I thought about telling her to make a run for her car, but I knew her multiple sclerosis had been flaring up, and she wouldn't make it. I knew if he caught her, he'd beat her to teach me a lesson.

I calmly told her to stop peeking out the blinds and call 911. I apologized, and then hung up! I was unraveling by the second, waiting for Shequita to pick-up the phone. After my third call, she announced Rick had escaped, and the police were escorting her back to the office.

I paused and said a silent prayer.

I was 100% certain; he'd keep coming back!

I kept saying over-and-over, "I'm a survivor. I'm not gon' give up. I'm gon' work harder, keep on surviving!" I convinced myself, I'd be back better and stronger than ever. But, who was I fooling? I was so tired of packing, moving, and running. "Lord, please give me the strength. I can't do it alone. Amen."

"I can do all things through Christ which strengtheneth me." (Philippians 4:13).

4

Fled!

According to the state's attorney, everyone was caught off-guard. No one expected Rick to come up with the bail money. They went on to say, "We want you to know we are working even more aggressively on the case."

"Okay," I replied. "Come in? No, that's not possible, I've moved out of the state, and I'd rather not say where. I must be honest; I've completely lost trust in the legal process and your office. I'm still pursuing the case, just not from Maryland. I will make any court dates necessary and see this through until the end."

For the last few days, I'd hardly slept more than 30 consecutive minutes. I found it difficult to eat, and bathing was a distant memory. My family was completely worried about me. It wasn't that I didn't *want* to sleep. On the contrary, I was being haunted over-and-over by the same nightmare: Rick stalking me, choking me, breaking in, and terrorizing me. Every door that creaked, every car that went by outside, or even a phone ringing would startle me. I'd wake up wide-eyed and hyperventilating.

I was coming unglued!

I thought this anxiety would subside once I left Maryland. At Tommy's house, I couldn't make it through the night without hiding out in the basement, in the fetal position, under a few throw rugs, and tucked away on the floor in the corner. I'd rationalized that if Rick broke into the house, he'd never find me in my makeshift fort and prayerfully not harm my innocent family.

For the life of me, I couldn't fathom how the prosecutor willingly bought his, "It was just a coincidence," story hook, line, and sinker.

It was just a coincidence that he was scheduled to leave town on the morning after he tried to kill me? He wasn't fleeing or alluding officers?

Riiight!

It was just a coincidence that he had $30,000 stashed in the trunk of his car? He was planning to invest in a start-up tech firm the day he was captured?

Okay!

It was just a coincidence that he lost his phone and didn't know the police wanted him to come back to the District for questioning?

It was just a coincidence that my eyes and neck showed immense signs of trauma, immediately after Rick exited my place on the night in question, and he had no idea what happened to me?

Everything the prosecutors told me appeared to be smoke and mirrors! I couldn't believe a thing they said.

"Denair, Rick wouldn't get bail. He would probably remain in jail until his trial!

Denair, you will more than likely never hear from Rick again!

Denair, you won't have to fear Rick, it's highly unlikely he'd violate his restraining order. He probably just disappeared!"

Everything the prosecutor told me would never happen, did happen! I saw the handwriting on the wall, and I'm glad I followed my instinct. If I'd waited just another 24 hours, Rick might have trapped me in my condo for the second time in seven days.

I dreaded leaving Maryland; I loved it there. Prior to escaping to Atlanta, I was in a perfect place in my life. I had a fabulous new condo, wonderful friends, an active church life, participation in several different ministries, and mentoring single moms.

I must admit working side-by-side with my brother was the icing on the cake. We represented the *Who's Who* of one of the most affluent communities in the world. Handling the legal affairs for celebrity athletes and political bigwigs that graced the Sunday morning talk shows was very fulfilling.

Now, back in Georgia, it just seemed that the grass wasn't as green, the sun didn't shine as brightly, and the air wasn't as fresh. Nothing was right. The distinguished, polished person known as Denair no longer existed. I was a shell of my former self. I wasn't eating, brushing my teeth, combing my hair, and bathing was an option I chose not to address. I had traded in my stilettos in for a pair of tattered flip-flops.

The only time I would leave my mother's house would be to hide-out at my sister, Lynnette's house. I would bolt from Lynnette's house, drive three and one-half miles to the local police precinct, make sure I wasn't being followed, turn back around, and hide out at Evelyn's house. The fact I could throw a rock from one of my sisters' front porches and hit the other sister's front door, went unnoticed in my mind.

What really scared me was the idea that Rick could show up at either Evelyn's or Lynnette's back door. He'd visited their homes briefly when he came to Atlanta for my daughter's college graduation three and one-half months earlier.

Things went from bad to worse (if that was possible) after I received a Facebook message from a childhood friend I'd hadn't spoken to in almost 25 years. Liz and I embraced virtually and chatted-up the good ole days in New York. We were having such an amazing time reminiscing; I felt the old Denair creeping out of the *Twilight Zone* I'd resided in the past few weeks.

Then it happened!

Liz told me I looked remarkably beautiful and asked whether I was married or dating anyone. I told her I was happily single after nearly being killed by an ex-boyfriend in a jealous rage. She was taken aback and wanted to know the details. Well, I only wanted to go back into my dark place and wrap-up the conversation. She persisted, and I eventually gave in. She was horrified after hearing what Rick had done and wanted to know where I met him. I replied, and said the guy was from Harlem, but I met him in Maryland.

She replied, "You know I'm from Harlem. I know everybody from Harlem."

In my mind, I'm like, "There is no way in the world she knows Rick." Nevertheless, I messaged her his street name back in the day, which was Boogie, and inboxed her a picture of him.

She asked for my phone number and said she'd call me in a few minutes.

Five minutes later, my cheerful, "Hey Girl" was met with a somber, "Hi." She said, "Denair I need you to listen to me and listen clearly. Boogie is a psychopath, and you're lucky to be alive."

My mind was going crazy! What did she know about him? Were we talking about the same detestable person?

She continued, long story short, "Denair, I highly recommend you never spend another second with that beast again. He is an absolute threat to you and your family. Twenty years ago, Boogie snuck up on an ex-girlfriend, choked her, wrapped her head in a plastic bag, and set her head on fire.

"Denair, I grew up around the corner from Boogie, and he's

always been violent. My girlfriend who is listening in on the other line was a best friend with the girl. She knows the facts as well as anyone. Would you like her to verify or confirm any part of the story?"

I declined, thanked her for the information, and excused myself from the call.

I thought, "My God! Why did you allow her to find me and share that horrific story?"

I was overcome with depression! I imagined myself being burnt beyond recognition and my family crying uncontrollably at my closed-casket funeral. I asked myself was this Rick's ultimate plan for me? I fell into deeper despair! I was determined to be more reclusive than ever!

I dropped out of college, exiting six credits shy of my degree. I completely abandoned collecting my tenant's rents, and all my bills were falling behind. I became obsessed with doing searches of me on the Internet, and each time, new information popped up! With the all the new technology of *Google Maps* and smart-phones, I knew it would only be a matter of time before he'd locate every property I owned. I'd simply be a sitting-duck by the first of every month. I told myself it was better to be safe than sorry. I simply walked away from my eight properties and allowed them to go into foreclosure.

Although I was hemorrhaging cash, I wasn't looking for a job, I wasn't concerned about my credit or looking to somehow recoup the $20,000 in upgrades I dumped into the Maryland condo.

There were no daily to-do lists being scribbled; no vision board or strategic planning being inked on a legal pad. It was like I checked out. The funny thing is that I could not even tell I was losing it.

Nothing about my current lifestyle was reminiscent of normalcy. Simple tasks like going to the grocery store, putting gas in my car, or taking out the trash were accompanied with lots of anxiety. I couldn't forecast whether I'd make it safely around the next corner. I had to stay on my Ps and Qs. I'd be looking around so much I made everyone around me nervous. Tomorrow wasn't promised!

In the back of my mind, I was haunted by the day Rick called in a hit on my daughter's abusive boyfriend from the passenger seat of my car. Rick barely knew my daughter, but yet in all of three minutes, he put in a call for things to be *dealt with.*

With Rick's life in the balance, facing major prison time, I couldn't help but think he'd pulled out all the stops to prevent me from testifying at his trial.

Words can't express how I felt when I boarded a flight from Atlanta to Maryland to participate in a pre-trial hearing. As I slid into my window seat, I gazed into the clouds, oblivious to all the noise on the aircraft. I wondered if it was too late to get off. I reasoned, I could just find a little cottage in the country and stay there until things died down. I reluctantly stayed on the plane after being reassured by Tommy I'd have a security detail in place when I landed at Baltimore-Washington International Airport. Expecting to see my brother, with one or two of his church buddies, I was blown away to learn I'd be escorted to the courthouse by three fully armed members of Baltimore SWAT.

When I arrived at the courthouse, I was greeted by three carloads of supporters, including a few off-duty officers who surrounded me. Although guarded, I was still petrified about seeing Rick in the courtroom. I was paranoid about just making it safely inside. I clutched Tommy's arm tightly while grabbing a stranger in close to my other side. Taking calculated steps between my entourage, I struggled to peer the rooftops of the surrounding buildings for snipers!

A bundle of nerves, I slowly entered courtroom B. with my head on a swivel. My eyes hazy and empty, sought the monster that tried to terminate my existence. My knees buckled, and I felt lightheaded at the thought of him rushing me. Fully expecting a confrontation, it was announced that Rick would be a no-show. I was mystified. The coward who attacked me from behind was nowhere to be found? I was an emotional wreck. I questioned whether prosecuting Rick was worth the emotional back-and-forth I was experiencing.

I headed back to Georgia, mortified at what I'd become. I questioned how I'd evolved into such a fragile being. My dad, a decorated New York City police officer, raised me to be fearless! I was repeatedly told if I ever ran away from a fight, he'd discipline me, then send me back out to fight—a battle, he reminded me, I had to win. Before becoming a cop, dad was a corrections officer in New York's notorious Rikers Island Correctional Facility. He was undaunted when confronted with dangerous situations and had ordered all five of his children to be the same.

Despite being very inactive in my life, my dad's message was crystal clear: confront fear head on!

I can recall the scorching summer day I'd won six straight games of handball, in my customary 30-inch length skirt. Due to Mom's religious beliefs, there was no such thing as wearing shorts or pants outside. It was cool, though; I got used to being different. So I had two choices. Option A: watch my peers, play day and night from my ninth-floor window, or Option B: throw on my ankle-length skirt and *Lotto* sneakers and commence to slaying all those who wanted to test my skills.

During my seventh game, Big Rich, an oversized neighborhood bully who weighed in at a comfortable 200 pounds, and stood just under six feet tall, began heckling at me, screaming, "Hey, Skirt Girl...Oh, Skirt Girl...Hey, Skirt Girl!" I thought to myself, "You don't have anything else to do with your time?"

Rich was a few years older than I, about 17. I just rolled my eyes and tried to ignore him. He lingered around the court with his pit bull on a thick linked chain and pronged choker collar.

For some reason, Big Rich gained a great deal of satisfaction, harassing a 15-year-old girl. He continued to agitate me with little to no response from me until he crossed the line by shouting, "Hey B! Don't ignore me. B! You hear me? I said, don't ignore me you skirt wearing B!"

In the middle of my serve, I simply dropped the blue handball and asked the loudmouth to repeat what he had said! He called me out my name again, this time, loud enough for the entire park to hear with a few other profanities.

Three full-court basketball games stopped, and you could hear a pin drop. I was so angry I couldn't even think straight!

Silly me. Rather than run across the street to the safety of my house or seek out my brothers, "Skirt Girl," rolled up her sleeves and darted off the court toward Rich.

In all of three seconds, I was three inches away from a ferocious pit bull that was lunging at me and the big bully who was preparing to swing.

With my left eye on the raging pit and the right eye on Big Rich's right hand, I took my fighting stance and stood my ground.

There was no fear and no panic. I only had thoughts of showing Rich that he couldn't mess with me. Moments before there was any contact, a bunch of guys who ditched their basketball game, ran over to separate us. After reprimanding Rich, an older man looked down at me and said, "Girl, what's wrong with you trying to fight this big guy and his dog?"

I was still hot and wanted justice for his disrespect.

Earlier in that summer, I received a rambling call from a neighbor that my best friend, Nicky was being chased down the street by eight so-called gangster girls in her projects. They were rivals from Washington Avenue Projects. I Immediately grabbed my sock full of D batteries and raced down nine flights of stairs, and across the train tracks. I frantically searched for Nicky.

By the time I found my home girl, she was cornered by a mob of 30-40 screaming people intending to do her great bodily harm. I burst through the crowd and made my way to Nicky, who was seconds away from an asthma attack. For the life of me, I couldn't understand why we always ended up in these situations. This wasn't my fight, but I knew I couldn't leave Nicky there alone to catch a beat down.

I jumped in front of my ride or die chick and eyeballed Cynthia, a girl nearly the size of Big Rich. I thought to myself, "If I clocked the biggest one first, maybe everyone else would back off." If that plan didn't work, we were both fast runners and God willing, could make it home alive that afternoon. I scanned the crowd in front of me and wondered why they were backing away slowly rather than attacking us. I was all of a buck-O-five soaking wet, and Nicky was thinner than I was.

I stole a glance behind me and noticed three of my siblings and nearly 60 Webster Projects neighbors, some whom I'd never spoken to, had joined my pursuit across enemy lines (the train tracks) to rescue Nicky. While it was okay to cross the tracks to play sports or attend an outdoor party (jam), it was an entirely different story when you crossed the lines to fight.

It was a relief to know my Webster Avenue *fame* had my back against the thugs from Washington Avenue Projects. Nevertheless, with or without the assistance I received, I was armed and ready to throw down for Nicky. I was fiercely loyal and fearless when it came to righting a wrong.

As I grew older, my determination to stand my ground landed me in jail. During my nine and one-half year marriage, I had been pinned-down, thrown, kicked, and slapped. My ex had escalated his abuse while I thought his actions would subside between counseling and weekly church attendance. His concealed drug addiction often caused him to lash out for no apparent reason. He was always annoyed by some unexpected activity that would set him off. The dysfunction became so normal I didn't even realize I was in an abusive relationship because I always fought back and stood up to him.

Sadly, I'd become immune to threats on my life. One day, he threw a ceramic dinner plate across the room and right by my head. As it flew across the living room from the kitchen, I watched it shatter into tiny pieces and did not flinch.

A few months later, while getting my four-year-old son and six-year-old daughter ready for school, I was viciously tossed into a sliding closet door. Whatever little thing had ticked him off that day would forever seal the fate of our marriage.

I staggered to my feet, absorbed a few more blows, and then scrambled to grab a three-foot wrought iron candelabra. Before I knew it, I could hear it crashing against his body over and over again until I wore myself out.

The neighbors heard the commotion at 7 a.m., and none of them came to my rescue. If I made it out the front door safely, I could have run up two flights of stairs to my auntie's apartment, but she was dealing with her own domestic issues. I reached for the phone and called 911 as he scurried out the door.

For the first time in nearly 10 years I called the police after being violently attacked and, in a shocking turn of events, I found myself in handcuffs for fending off my abuser.

As I refused to exhibit fear during my ex's attacks, I also made it a point not to show any signs of weakness as I sat in a cell surrounded by 40 other inmates, for nearly 48 hours.

Although I wasn't proud of my actions, I felt absolutely justified. In my opinion, he'd gotten what he deserved. I celebrated the fact that I was a survivor. My only regret was that I hadn't stood up for myself and my children sooner.

Years later, as I reflected, I questioned whether my fearlessness on behalf of Nicky and toward my ex was simply fool-hearty. I told myself when it came to my family, (Nicky and my kids) I'd do whatever it took to ensure their safety.

After literally escaping my volatile marriage, I vowed to become a voice for the voiceless. I promised I'd do all I could to protect defenseless women and enhance the lives of single moms. I wanted to educate and empower them about the ills of abuse. I am a judgment-free ear and a shoulder for them to cry on.

I'd become an unyielding advocate in the real sense of the word. I achieved multiple certifications in domestic violence and intimate partner violence and continuing education on the psychology of children involved. Becoming a fierce women's rights attorney would be my ideal accomplishment.

To look at myself now, just a few months after Rick's attack, I was a broken, empty vessel. My overwhelming depression prompted me to spend more-and-more time apart from those who loved me the most. They did not know how to help me; they had never seen me this way.

I wanted to apologize to my sisters for behaving so weird, but I was embarrassed for myself and agonized in self-pity, questioning every decision I had ever made.

I did have some good days as I struggled to regain my emotional footing. However, I was still looking over my shoulder and crying through sleepless nights, staying two-nights here and three-nights there.

My transformation was slowly impacting my personal hygiene and caused Evelyn to take drastic measures of her own. When my sister came home from work, she barged into her room with some ammunition to combat my funk!

She announced she had a special treat for me by singing my name in syllables to add to the surprise. I closed my eyes and held out my hands while smiling from ear to ear, exposing my dimples in anticipation of an amazing gift. My sisters and I were always picking up things for each other from *Wal-Mart* or the mall.

As I heard the bag rattling, my excitement was growing more and more. I started to peek, but Evelyn said, "Not yet, Dee." I could feel the covers moving as she was arranging something at the end of the bed. I called out like a five-year-old, "Is it a new dress, a pair of pumps, or tickets to a show?" The suspense was killing me. She finally yelled, "You can look now!" As I opened my eyes, I furrowed my brows in confusion. Evelyn was trying to hold back the laughter as she pointed to the array of *Bath and Body Works* products spread out. She handed me some scented soap, creamy lotion, and a body spray. And if that wasn't enough to get the job done, she had a care package with a shower cap, toothbrush, toothpaste, deodorant, and some dental floss.

Was I that bad? Probably so. I couldn't even get upset. I eventually started laughing after I took a quick whiff toward my right armpit. My mom always says laughter is the best medicine, and boy did I need a huge dose.

Evelyn's message was crystal clear: I had to pull it together and rebuke this spirit of hopelessness. The Bible says, "For God hath not given us the spirit of fear; but of power, and of love, and of a sound mind." (2 Timothy 1:7).

I desperately wanted to get back to my bright, bubbly self. "Lord help me, please!"

I claimed it was time to live life to the fullest!

Just days after Evelyn's stand up comedy bit, I received a call at 11:59 p.m. from Tommy. Although it was late, surprisingly he was full of life. Our family was known for going to bed earlier than most, and for me, dark meant to sleep. Typically, I would not even pick-up the phone at that time of night, but the phone just kept ringing-and-ringing. When I saw Tommy's name flashing across the caller ID that lit up the room, I assumed it was some extreme emergency.

It had been weeks since I'd spoken to Tommy. From what Mommy indicated, he was coping with his own overwhelming situations, which were now compounded by my horrific attack and absence from running the firm. His two upscale restaurants were currently being renovated, and daily-unexpected costs were spiking out of control. The tenants occupying his 13 investment properties were playing hide-n-seek, every time the first of the month rolled around.

To make matters worse, the acting office manager was suffering from severe health challenges and was forced to work half days or call out sick.

Although he never expressed it to me, I'm sure Tommy was guilt-ridden for not being able to protect me from Rick. We were both in a world of hurt, 700 miles apart from each other.

To hear Tommy's voice, five octaves higher than his normal baritone caught me off-guard. His excitement was contagious, despite the sleep in my eyes and the bass in *my* voice. He didn't apologize for waking me and blurted out, "We *is* going to be rich! We're going to be rich! This is what we've been praying for our entire lives." I told myself either Tommy hit the lottery or he's worse-off than Mommy and I both imagined.

"Denair, if I could show you a way to make additional income, would you want me to tell you?" Without hesitation, an exuberant "Yes!" rang out. "Great!" Tommy chanted. He urgently continued as if time was running out and I had made it to the next round of *Jeopardy*. "If I could help you save and get paid on all your essential products and services, would you want me to tell you?" "Yes, Yes!" This was exciting! "Great," Tommy said as if we were approaching the final bonus round. "If I could introduce you to six and seven figure income earners who could show you a system that was easy to do, easy to learn, and easy to duplicate, would you be willing to get started with me?"

"Yes, Yes, Yes!" I sang. "Great, give me your credit card. I need to put you in the system right away. I knew you were a winner, Dee. Let's get this money!" Tommy exclaimed, "...and begin creating residual income for our family."

Tommy was rambling so much; I knew he drank the *Kool-Aid.* But he was someone I knew, loved, and trusted his entire life, and confidently relied heavily on the fact that he would never introduce me to something that he didn't personally believe in.

He whispered, "I'm sitting with a millionaire right now. Dee, the guy works less than two hours a day, uses the word, 'Bidness,' and he is running circles around my good attorney income." Tommy blew me away when he said the guy only has a high school diploma, and he's enjoying the lifestyle of any high paid entertainer or athlete.

I did the math real quick. Between Tommy and myself, we were educated and trained in broadcasting, real estate, English, law, and certifications in the title industry, mortgage banking, foreclosure prevention, and education. I told myself, "I'm a shrewd businesswoman," and assessed if other everyday people could succeed then, I knew Tommy and I could change the game. We had a work ethic out of this world, and a never say, "Can't" or have a quit mentality!

I said, "Tommy, have you checked this guy out?" The last thing I needed was another guy blowing smoke. He responded by saying,

"Dee, he's legit. In addition to the plush mansion I'm sprawled out in right now, he owns another one next door as well. He's definitely living the Life of Riley.

"Here's the deal, in a nutshell, Dee. The company works with a number of Fortune 500 and 100 companies, marketing products and services that everyone *needs* and can never pay off, even if they were a billionaire. The products practically sell themselves, but he's willing to mentor us until we're making six-figures a month, working two hours a day. As a matter of fact, I'll be hanging out with him at his house for the next few days. I need you to get here as soon as you can!"

Certainly, Tommy was mistaken when he said he needed me in Maryland. Didn't he know I was in hiding and in fear of my life? Couldn't I just stay in the comfort of Evelyn or Lynnette's living room and create this wealth?

I'd be walking directly into the line of fire if I returned to Maryland. Unable to go back to sleep, I Googled a few of the success stories that Tommy mentioned and found quite a bit of information on them and the company.

What was impressive was that many of the individuals who had acquired wealth through the business looked a lot like me, people of color. There were also many women in the top levels of the company. One, in particular, was in her early 30s, had two young children, and was a single mom.

I began to sound like Tommy, saying "This is an opportunity of a lifetime!" Our days in the Webster Projects were long behind us, but we always believed we had much more to accomplish. We were standing on the shoulders of so many giants who made sacrifices to allow us to obtain a better life. It has always been our family's model to give back and bless as many people as possible along our journey as well. And this may just be the vehicle to do so.

The next day, one of the top producers in the company personally called me. I simply stated, "If my brother is all-in, no need convincing me. I'm all in as well!"

While I was taken in with the new business opportunity and all the new energy it was injecting in me, I couldn't lose sight of the critical issue at hand. Rick was still loose on the streets, and I was not sold on returning to meet his wrath. No one knew exactly where he was, but chances were, he was staying close to the Maryland, DC, or Virginia area. That's where his people were: his daughter, his homies from work, and other cohorts that he ran with.

The more I left messages for the prosecutor's office, the less I received return calls. I was beginning to feel like the case was going cold. Maybe being in Maryland, doing weekly pop-up visits would remind them that I was not going away. Out of site, out of mind. Yes, they needed to see and feel my presence to understand I will aggressively be involved at every step of this case. My grandmother always said the squeaky wheel gets the oil.

Rick needed to be held accountable for what he took from me physically, psychologically, emotionally, financially, and spiritually. How many other women would become his victims? I'm convicted that God spared my life for such a time as this. Who would stand up for us? If not me, then who?

When Rick strangled me, he killed the incredible momentum Tommy and I were building at the practice. We gave everything and never subscribed to taking shortcuts or cutting corners. We had worked together for many years and countless, grueling hours, sacrificing our time, family events, resources, sleep, and our health. Participating in community functions, weekend activities, and working holidays was not uncommon. We were willing to go above and beyond to create and maintain a thriving business.

Tommy and I were on the map after acting as treasurer for Prince George's County newly elected chief executive. At the time, Prince George's County was the fourth richest county in the United States. Our faces were plastered on television several times throughout the day and on commercials highlighting the legal and title services we offered.

The *Congressional Black Caucus* solicited our expertise as well. A state senator heard of our work assisting many large congregations and conducting workshops to save homes. We tailored a presentation titled, *Foreclosure Prevention Strategies* at their annual legislative conference. We were prominent, active leaders in business and the community. And somewhere deep down, I wanted to create something great with Tommy again. I felt responsible for the immense pressure he and the practice were under due to my abrupt escape after my attack.

My mother and two sisters feared for my safety and begged me to stay in Atlanta. They wanted to keep a close eye on me. However,

I decided to return to Maryland and rescue the brother who'd rescued me so many times before. Tommy and I had a unique relationship like that. Not many siblings would totally leave their entire lives behind to work, support, or risk their own life for each other. Although I'm equally close with to the rest of my siblings, Tommy and I have worked the longest and closest in business together.

Although it seemed ridiculous, I told myself, I'd take on the role of protector like I'd done so many times before. My brother needed me right away, so I was dispatching my fears in hopes of alleviating the incredible stress that was weighing him down. If everything worked according to plan, we'd be the *Dynamic Duo* again. Maybe this was the miracle we both needed.

My only challenge was avoiding Rick, whose residence was three miles north of Tommy and two miles south of our new mentor's house. Unless I left the area, I'd eventually bump into Rick at the local *Starbucks, Chick fil A, Target*, or supermarket.

I packed my bags in haste, taking only enough clothes for a few weeks. Rolling out my purple designer luggage set to the driveway, solidified my "ready or not, here I come" mentality. I jumped in the car and set out to make my fortune. I prayed my impulsive plan didn't backfire and leave me regretting my decision.

As I blazed a trail up Interstate 85 North at my regular racetrack speed, I tried to focus on all the beautiful trees, the vast blue sky, and the sun that represented the beginning of a brand new day. I loved taking long road trips; it's when I have the most intimate time with God. Observing all of nature and His bountiful creations always puts me in a relaxed state of mind. However, anxiety kept sprouting as I struggled to repress it.

Just at that moment, I noticed the gift bags that my cousins Gloria and Lisa brought when they came to help me pack after the attack. It had been two months, and there they sat at the foot of the passenger seat. I kept meaning to open them, but my depression kept getting the better of me. The bags were beautiful, laced with a host of colorful streamers.

My cousins were always treating me like their little sister. They even threw me a surprise birthday party once that could have easily been mistaken for a grand wedding. The lavishly decorated room sat on a lake in the exclusive Poconos Mountains. They went all-out with a DJ, catered food, party favors, and exquisite china settings graced the elegant tablecloths. I thought the night could not get any better until I saw an enormous cake rolled out that had my picture on it. Just as I was getting ready to hit the dance floor, Gloria announced there was one more surprise. "What else could it be?" I thought. The next thing I knew, my life from infancy to the most memorable times I could remember were projected on a drop-down screen. The video was compliments of my gifted cousin, Debra; she is the techy one of the family.

As I reached down for the gifts, I was confident that whatever was inside would bring me joy. Gloria's bag was first. Out came a large envelope that said, "We are praying for you, Denair." The card inside was insulated with lots of cash. Although the money was absolutely needed, the sentiment expressed was even more precious than pure gold.

I automatically recognized the face on the CD. It was Kirk Franklin. He is one of my favorite gospel artists. Although he is most popular for bringing contemporary gospel to the mainstream, his testimony expressed through his lyrics captured me.

Lisa purchased his new CD titled, *Hello Fear*. I ripped off the packaging in seconds, guiding the disc into the player. The soothing melody instantly drew me in, but I did not anticipate the range of emotions that flooded my soul as I meditated on the words. My wounded spirit sank in the driver's seat, as I heard my own thoughts resounding through the speakers.

God is such an on-time God. I listened to that CD for the next 13-14 hours as I wrestled with my own demons of fear while heading to Maryland.

Many of the songs mirrored my fears, depression, loneliness, and even concerns about dying. However, the resounding message was consistent with rebuking those concerns, disappointing my depression, refusing to fall victim to the lies the devil perpetrated (with my help) that made me feel defeated. The verses introduced me to healing, mercy, and grace while challenging me to live and not die. As I hid the words in my heart, as I hit repeat over-and-over for hours on end, my brokenness began to heal. I was empowered by each promise I heard. *Hello Fear* the very first song, is without a doubt my favorite. The lyrics denounced my fears and, after listening to the song 200 times, I found myself crying, singing, and shouting the chorus as it strengthened my courage.

Hello, Fear!

Never again will I love you

My heart it refuses to be your home

No longer your prisoner

Today I remember

Apart from you is where I belong

And never again will I trust you

I'm tired of fighting it's been way too long

No longer your prisoner

Today I remember

Who I was and now it's gone

Farewell Goodbye So long!!!

I was truly a woman on a mission. I drove the entire 14 hours without making a *Cinnabon* run, pushed through my powernap urges, and dreadfully drove by dozens of discount outlets, I was on gas-and-go mode, laser focused and razor sharp. I drove straight through the night racing to my two o'clock date with destiny, and I would not miss it.

I divorced fear, got engaged to inspiration, and committed to happiness. To reaffirm my new found freedom, I texted myself a reminder saying, "Dear future, I'm now ready!"

I was going home to conquer!

5

Living Room Wealth!

"The question isn't who is going to let me; it's who is going to stop me."—Ayn Rand

I'd driven 14 straight hours, dodged speed traps, and crossed over the Mason-Dixon Line for what Tommy described as an opportunity of a lifetime! The thought of how far I'd fallen was the motivation behind scratching and clawing to make it out of that deep ditch!

It was just approaching 1:30 p.m. as I pulled up to the gated, manicured estates. Although I was early, my enthusiasm propelled me to key in the code Tommy sent me. As the gate opened, I canvassed the community with its cobblestone driveways and grand double-doored entrances. The pillared homes easily sat on an acre of land. The oversized windows with no treatments obscuring my view, allowed me to peer right through the luxurious mansions with winding grand staircases.

As I pulled up to the address on my GPS, I wiped my sweaty palms on my jeans. I smacked a piece of *Trident* in my mouth and realized my hair must look a mess too. I reached to the backseat, threw on a cap, and quickly freshened up my lips. Sneaking a peek in the mirror, I cleaned the sleep out of my eyes before swinging the door open. My swollen feet were relieved to reach my destination, as I gracefully headed up the walkway.

Seconds after the bell chimed, a beautiful, pleasant, petite woman invited me in and before I could fully introduce myself. She instructed me to go through the dining room to get to the den. As I approached the room, I heard laughter from multiple voices. The man looked up and said, "What's up, Dee? Come in." I immediately recognized the voice as the highly successful man Tommy introduced me to over the phone.

The handsome young millionaire greeted me as if we were long lost cousins. I was even more blown away by his laidback attire, which consisted of basketball shorts and Michael Jordan flip-flops. I felt right at home as his personality made me think of my brother. He went on-and-on, about how much I could make in the business and then with excitement welcomed me to the team.

I couldn't speak or think. I didn't want to seem too excited. But secretly I was like, "Girl, I'm on my way. No more 800, 866, or 877 numbers calling me (my voicemail stayed full)."

This was the break I'd prayed for, but I had to keep it real with my new mentor. I started off with, "This is the deal: I don't have any time or money to be playing with this thing! I just lost a ton of money on renovations on a condo that I had to abandon. And the money I used to get started in the business wasn't even mine to blow. My tenant just made that deposit to me, so technically, it belonged to *Bank of America*. All of my savings had been wiped out on a personal situation I'm dealing with."

"So what's up," I asked? "Is this thing really above board? I see it's working for you, but can it work for me?" I had nothing left, and I needed this thing to work!

In all honesty, after what I'd been through, I wanted some type of guarantee or proof this wasn't some fly-by-night or get-rich-quick scheme.

He responded by going on the Internet and pulling up the success profiles of two women who were his mentors when he broke into the business 36 months earlier.

The first video I viewed was of a young single mom of a four and nine-year-old boys. I was stunned at how someone younger than I was earning six-figures a month from the comfort of her home that would make Oprah envious.

As the camera toured her illustrious six-bedroom, 11-bath, 18,000-square foot mansion, which, oh, by the way, had seven fireplaces, I felt ridiculous coveting my pocket-sized California Closet just three months ago.

I was blown away as I viewed story-after-story of individuals who were no longer living paycheck-to-paycheck. Incredibly, another woman was able to start her own clothing line that now boasts inclusion in all the upscale boutiques around the country. Her wealth also afforded her the time and resources to spend all the precious time she wanted with her children and husband on lavish vacations around the world.

If these inexperienced ladies, who were practically carrying toddlers on their hips, could achieve this success, there was no reason I couldn't do the same.

Like a convert at a church revival, I raised both hands and yelled, "I'm in!"

If things worked out, I'd be able to move into my own mansion and possibly bless a lot of other people along the way, especially women. Was I really foolish enough to think I could do it too? If success were easy, then everyone would be successful! I *had* to try. If it didn't work, I could always go back to being broke!

I rolled up my sleeves and said, "So what's next?" Although Tommy had officially enrolled me a few weeks prior, I was not really in until that moment. As we sat for the next few hours, we scrolled through my phone and reached out to a lot of contacts about this not so secret something that could change their lives as well.

I was like a brand new baby, clinging to every sound and movement its mother made. Call-after-call I listened as the questions never deviated. My new mentor asked prospects if they had a cellphone. All said they did. He asked if they had cable. A few replied, "Bootleg," but that's not the point, they all were watching TV!

He asked if they used credit or debit cards, and the final sure shot was if they used lights and took baths, which certainly was, "Yes and yes!" The follow-up got their attention every time, which was, "Do you get paid when you use them?" And of course, the answer was "No!"

The presentation went on as my mentor continued with, "Would you like me to solve that problem for you?" He always kept it real hood. He was not one of those uptight scholarly types. He would cut right to the chase and say, "Here's the deal...

"We get a small check every time we pay our monthly electric, cable, cellphone, and gas bills, and it doesn't stop there. And how would you like to get paid every time your mother, sister, cousins, church members, or church building paid bills as well?" He had me hook, line, and sinker. I was gonna use that one!

But really, you *could* get paid on buildings, and probably blocks, and entire cities. This was bigger than I thought. And instantly I realized so much more was possible!

In a nutshell, we got paid to share information on everyday products and services that people had to pay every day anyway! Using our net*work* to help build our net *worth* just like *Facebook*'s, Mark Zuckerberg, was a stroke of genius. Using social media was a classic model.

There's no limit to the amount of money you can make or the people you can bless with these monthly savings.

He said this wasn't rocket science. You simply get a cousin or neighbor to purchase their next cellphone or cable services from one of our partner companies, like *Verizon, T-Mobile, Sprint, DISH* or *DirecTV*. Then bam! You receive a monthly thank-you check for as long as the customer pays their bill.

I thought this was truly amazing! Getting paid every Friday and on the 15th of the month was exciting! My mentor mentioned something I was not familiar with, but I knew it had to be good because he kept repeating it. To myself, I kept saying, "Residual? What's that?" He finally circled back to it, explaining it's the same way songwriters get paid for a song they wrote one time. Doing something one time and getting paid over-and-over for it years later sure sounded like a hit to me.

Just to confirm the savings were really there, I went online to compare what the company had to offer. I never thought of saving on my utility bills like I could at the pump, by just going to lower priced gas stations. Who knew?

I quickly went online and switched all of my personal services that didn't say "Pay to the order of... Denair." It was liberating!

Gas and electric switched! Cell phone carrier, check! Security system, done! Despite being brand-new to this, it seemed simple enough, but I couldn't explain it if I tried.

So I just said the same thing Tommy said to me, which was, "You wanna be rich, join my business? I'm hanging out with millionaires now and they are teaching me how to earn at their income levels; wanna learn?" That's called duplication. If I wanted to get what was gotten, I had to do what was done. I was the epitome of ignorance on fire.

Before I knew it, I had a full-fledged organization (that's what they told me anyway). I really didn't understand any of the terminology or the back-office stuff. I did, however, know how to spend the money that came every Friday and on the 15th.

I was on my way to getting paid like those women in the videos, and it was all legal. It appeared this business opportunity would be like taking candy from a baby.

And, why wouldn't it be?

- Virtually everyone on the planet over the age of thirteen has a cellphone
- I couldn't think of a soul who wouldn't want to lower their electric bill
- The company was launching a new line of health products (coffee, tea, and smoothies) that accelerated weight loss

How could anyone lose? It was a win-win for customers and business partners.

My only regret was not learning of this lucrative option years earlier. I asked myself, how much easier would life have been for my daughter, son, or mother if I'd learned about this $250 opportunity sooner.

I reflected on my life and thought about many of the decisions I'd made based on money, or should I say, the lack of money. Would I have stayed in a bad marriage as long if I had the resources to provide for my children? Would I have moved so many times out of the need to survive? Had I been living according to my purpose?

As I continued scrolling over the names of people who needed more options and financial breakthroughs, there appeared to be no shortage of friends and family members living well below their potential. I decided I would just throw out a lifeline and pull in anyone who grabbed hold of it.

I decided I'd start reaching out to people who owed me money, then move on to clients with significant past due balances with the law firm; *they* certainly had cash flow issues.

For crying out loud, I'd at least expected those who owed me a few grand to offer more than icy silence. Sometimes I couldn't tell if the call dropped or they were just dead silent. Were people obsessed with being broke? They would say:

Pyramid!

You know it's a scam!

Not interested; not now, not tomorrow, not ever.

Really? One of those things?

Pyramid!

Won't work.

Don't have the money.

My cousin tried that.

Thanks, but no thanks. Don't call back! I like you; I'll get you your money, but don't call back.

After the first 50 calls, those were just some of the more *positive* comments I heard from people. And I knew most of them were *trying to make a dollar out of 15 cents*, just like I was. Did they enjoy the struggle? I couldn't understand why nobody wanted to get started as quickly as I did.

I thought to myself, "Maybe I was moving too fast and saying something wrong."

Then my MLM mentor proceeded to pick up my phone dial the next prospect on my list and delivered the most flawless elevator pitch I'd ever heard. In all of 60-seconds, I had a well-to-do husband and wife on my team. Yes, I needed his help. I just assumed if he could do it, well so could I. Maybe, I should stop telling my sad story? Hmm...

Well, I needed to be going. I had no idea I was there for four hours. I had learned more in those few hours than I had in all my years in school and in life. College degree or not, this guy was a real genius.

That was it, most of society was just taught the wrong way, and it can't be reversed overnight. Well, tomorrow would be a new beginning for me.

By the time I made it to Tommy's house, I was exhausted. I put in a full 18 hours with no sleep, and only had a bag of chips a few hours earlier on the road. But I needed to do all three hours of what our company called *University* that my mentor kept talking about. This is training the company put together to assist with winning in the business.

I had to at least *begin* the classes. I needed a jumpstart the very next day. I kept nodding off and my eyes were burning. I was slumped over in the most awkward positions, still with my *MacBook* on my lap. When I got up in the morning, my neck was cramped, feet were still swollen, I was hungry enough to eat a cow, but I got my University session done!

I grabbed something to eat, dashed to pick Tommy up from the airport, then headed back to our mentor's home. I was going to be the star student that day. Tommy and I were like two little kids in a candy store. Excited to see each other, it had almost been three months without dreading the dark shadow that caused our parting, or catching up on Tommy's weeklong excursion; we just focused on our newfound freedom. I blurted out, "Tommy, I stayed up all-night doing my classes! I don't feel like I know everything yet, but at least I understand the verbiage and can speak a little more confidently. This is completely different from anything I've ever done. Do you think it can really work?"

"Absolutely," Tommy chimed in before I could finish my thought.

As we sped past our office, which happened to be three lights from our mentor's home, we both burst out laughing. It would be there when we were done; first things first. It felt so good laughing with Tommy again, just like old times.

Instead of parking on the street like I had yesterday, Tommy said, "Dee, pull up in front of the house!" I could tell by his tone he had done this before. This is the first time we would be visiting our mentor's house together, but it was definitely not the last. As

Tommy aggressively rang the doorbell, I stood back thinking it was too early to invite ourselves over.

Ironically, a few minutes later, half asleep and in his robe, our mentor opened the door. He was not as pleasant as he was yesterday. "Dag, man, it's 7:30 in the morning," he said. With his chipper voice and dimples showing, Tommy said, "Wake up. Let's get going. Time to make the donuts." Tommy walked by him without apologizing as I followed, barely saying good morning. A mumbled, "What's up, Dee?" came from my mentor, followed by, "He's crazy, and I guess you are too." As he closed the door, he said, "I'll be back in a few, let me get dressed."

Tommy walked right into the den, unescorted as if it were his house. "This is bananas," I thought. As Tommy and I waited, he said, "He's cool, right? He's my main man. We are really doing it, Dee, and he is just like me: no games, all about making this money. Pay attention to everything; don't try to take notes or anything, just listen to how he explains everything. We are in school!"

Thirty-minutes had passed before our host reappeared. He seemed a little bit more like the man I'd met the day before, but not fully, as he was still a little groggy. He asked Tommy if he brought him a coffee at least. Tommy said, "No, but we will go back out shortly." Tommy turned to me and whispered, "He's not really a morning person." Our mentor jumped in saying, "That's right, I'm not used to jumping out of my sleep when an alarm clock tells me to. I wake up when my eyes open! But your brother is my new alarm clock. Does he ever sleep? He's here early in the morning, and then stays all-day and night. He said he has an office down the street, but I don't believe him because he's never there."

"Ouch," I thought. But Tommy just kept on smiling and chuckled, "Later for that office right now!" It was almost 9 a.m., and Tommy's cell started blowing up as usual. Without looking down at the screen, he just passed it to me. Yep, not much had changed. It was the office reminding him of his appointments for the day. When I answered the call, Shequita was surprised and asked when I got to Maryland? I replied, "Yesterday," as she continued with, "I hope you're coming in too. There's so much to do around here. Where *are* you guys? His appointment is on the way, and it's already been rescheduled twice."

"We will be there shortly; we are right down the block."

"At that man's house again?" Shequita raised her voice and sucked her teeth. "One of you please get here and meet this client. It's too early for this on a Monday, and you know I'm not feeling well. Glad you are back!"

Was I back? Was I going to be running the office again or making my fortune? I relayed the message to Tommy, but he didn't pay me much attention. As I shook my head and rolled my eyes at him, I thought, "What have I gotten myself into?"

Tommy was already calling people and handing the phone to our mentor after giving a brief introduction. It went something like this. "Hi, did I catch you at a good time?" No matter what the reply, Tommy continued with a rousing, "Great! I'm working with a former barber who has a high school diploma and makes more money than any lawyer or brain surgeon I know. He is helping me to do the same. Can you speak with him for a few minutes? Do you want to be rich?" Then Tommy would just hand the phone to our mentor. And that's how it went for the next few hours.

The office stopped ringing Tommy's phone and called me instead. "Tommy, we *have* to go!" I heard my voice piercing for the hundredth time. "Dee, you go to the office," he said. "I will be there in a little while. Meet with the clients until I get there. They will be happy to meet with 'Ms. Hudge-jins.' They like you better anyway." That was our little inside joke because some of the clients would say my name incorrectly. We would always get a good laugh out of it, but Tommy was just trying to get me to go to the office for him.

As I walked to my car I told myself I would only meet with that one client; then I would leave. Before I knew it, it was 4:30 p.m. and I was drained. As I finally escaped to the bathroom, a familiar face was walking toward the office. "Oh, my God. I heard what happened to you. Are you okay? Are you back for good?" Pastor Johnson was getting a loan modification done on his home and was responsible for us doing workshops in the community churches. His wife had recently passed away, and we grew rather close during that time. I nodded and gave a quick hug, then ran into the bathroom. As I returned to the office Pastor Johnson called out, "They said I will be seeing *you* today." I just sighed with a smile and said, "Please step into the first conference room. I will be right with you. I was done with Pastor Johnson by 5:25 p.m. As he exited, I called out, "Please turn the phones off for the day."

Still no Tommy. I was so busy, and I didn't have time to keep calling him. Anyway, this was the last time this was going to happen! I had a brief meeting with the staff as they all had concerns and unresolved issues. Tired and hungry, I forgot I hadn't eaten all day. I grabbed my purse, said goodnight, and headed to *Chipotle*. It was right under our office. As the door closed behind me, I heard a voice say "See you tomorrow."

"Not if I can help it," I replied with a slight laugh, but I was serious.

Walking into *Chipotle* was never an in-and-out type of thing. There were long lines wrapped around the entire building sometimes. My choices were limited as a vegetarian, and I wanted something healthy and fulfilling. As I leaned against the wall looking through the transparent windowpane, I thought I recognized Rick's car. It was a white *Dodge Charger* with distinctive detailing. I stepped out of the line to get a closer look, but it was out of my view by then. Was it him or was I just worked up from the busy day? I tried not to focus on it and moved closer to place my order.

I got back in the car, surveying the entire parking lot, which was surrounded by lots of other restaurants and stores. I jumped in the car, locked my doors, and drove as quickly as possible to update Tommy.

When I got back to our mentor's house, it looked like they were sitting in the same positions from earlier that morning. Tommy grabbed my *Chipotle* and started eating it. Before I could say anything, Tommy asked what had taken me so long to get back. "Let's get going on your list." I started to tell him about the car but didn't want to get into it in front of anyone else. As I picked up a fork to eat some of my own food. Tommy said, "What's wrong, Dee? Sorry, I ate your food. I was so hungry!"

I said, "It's not that; I think I saw Rick's car in our office parking lot." Tommy said it was probably not him and kept working. "Come on, Dee; it's okay. You're with me. I got you." Our mentor asked what was going on. "Who is Rick?" Without giving all of the details, I gave a brief overview of the attack. Our mentor blurted out, "Dee, what kind of knuckleheads you dealing with? How long did you date him? Was he roughing you up the entire time? Dag, what did you do to make him want to kill you?"

I said, "It's not like that. He never hit me during the entire time I dated him, which was nine months. As a matter of fact, we never even really argued. It was when I broke up with him that he came to my house and tried to kill me a week later." Our mentor asked if we were home alone. I said, "Yes, but the contractors saw him and had just left seconds before." Our mentor said, "Yeah, he's a crazy one alright. Witnesses and he still went on with the plan? That dude was planning on leaving town and for you to be dead!" He continued with, "You know I'm from the streets? Trust me, he ain't coming up in here and if he does he won't be ready for what I got."

Okay, so now that I felt safe at Fort Knox, I could relax (for a while anyway). Tommy went right back to business and said, "So who are we calling next?" Our mentor jumped in and said, "Y'all have any more crazy family members like both of you, that are hard workers with thick skin?"

I said, "I know just the person."

My first prospect I called on day two, was my 21-year-old son, Shon, a hard working third-year college student. Shon had just moved off campus and was taking odd jobs to supplement his *Ramen Noodle* diet and gas up his 1984 *Camry*. An independent-minded kid majoring in business, Shon consistently refused my financial support. Just seven days earlier, he excitedly called and told me how he'd painted the entire interior and exterior of a two-story home in just two days for $75. I thought, "Poor kid." He thought he'd hit the lottery. Yep, he certainly sounded like a person in need of a financial opportunity. Before I finished with my pitch, he said, "Mom, multiple jobs are for multiple people. This is what I've been praying for. Sign me up!"

Next up was my BFF, Ronda. Although she was a well-paid nurse, I knew Ronda was running herself into the ground, working day and night, then night and day. She often complained about how she missed being home with her husband and her four-year-old son. Missing his school plays, basketball games on the weekend, and church at times was wreaking havoc on her family life. Ronda gave me a vivacious, "Yes!"

I called my sister, Evelyn. She rushed me off the phone indicating she'd call me once she finished processing paper work for each of the five attorneys she subcontracted herself out to. Evelyn was one of the hardest workers I knew. As an 18-year-old she was working 65 hours a week at a major firm on Wall Street. While the money was beyond excellent, she was often agitated and made for an awful lunch date. Fast forward 20 years, and she was still grinding herself to death, putting in insane hours. Too busy to talk, she texted me her credit card information and said she was in!

For the next 12 hours, Tommy and I emailed, texted, and called every person we'd ever dated, every tenant that ever paid late, and those we had to evict. We called former clients struggling to prevent foreclosures, those who were contemplating divorce due to financial hardship, and any person who'd ever uttered the word "entrepreneur" in our midst.

Thanks to great tutelage, the 15-second pitch we were delivering was beginning to pique the interests of everyone, from the well-to-do to those struggling and almost on welfare.

Too excited to go home, Tommy and I decided to grab a power nap right on the steel living room floor. It was 2:30 a.m. Tommy and I had slept for all of 45 minutes before we were back at it again. We headed for our laptops to draft letters to pastors, overwhelmed attorneys, and business owners whom the state of Maryland indicated recently filed for bankruptcy protection.

Tommy and I finally left before the sun came up to sleep in real beds, if even for an hour or two.

On day three, I'd crafted what I called a *90-day Blueprint to Wealth*. My formula didn't require a doctorate; it just required that I work harder, faster, and smarter than I had ever done before. Although I was still learning, the momentum was contagious.

Besides, this is the same way college kids are taught to grind. Work, work, work, take spring break, then winter break. Then they'd turn right back around and start the grind all over again. They are not even guaranteed jobs! And what about their mounting loans, especially in today's economy?

Yes, earning MBAs in university were necessary. However, this time, our grind would lead to *Massive Bank Accounts*!

I was fired up, and my passion would demonstrate I was prepared to *lose* it all to *gain* it all.

Another way we searched for new business partners was by having Private Business Receptions (PBRs). This was normally done in a home setting, and we had no problem packing out our mentor's dream home with prospects. This is the same place Tommy was tricked into attending a PBR just weeks before, and it was ideal for expanding the vision for those who were seeking a real financial blessing.

Our mentor was always dropping nuggets on us like, "If you help enough people, get what they want in life, you'll have an overflowing of things you desire in your life."

Another jewel he dropped was, "You're not *selling* the opportunity. Rather, you're *sharing* this blessing with others."

To be completely honest, it all sounded rather spiritual to me. The principles I learned my entire life as the daughter of a Bible evangelist and the granddaughter of a reverend was sharing the good news. I can recall handing out religious tracts for hours on end as a child, to total strangers, and when they refused, I was not deterred from moving on with my mission.

I quickly surmised that if I were going to be successful in this industry, I'd have to adopt the mindset! I told myself that when I truly focused on people's needs, rather than pushing the opportunity, filling the room would be as easy as 1, 2, 3! So I asked myself:

- *Whom do I care about?*
- *To whom can I gift this opportunity?*
- *Whom would I like to see live a better life?*

It was common for Tommy and me to pack the house night after night with 50-75 warm market prospects. However, the real person who stole the show was our mentor. He was extremely skillful in the art of delivering the opportunity.

The guests could not tell if they were at a revival, in a courtroom, or listening to Al Sharpton.

His closing appeal was so compelling that two-thirds of the people in attendance simply could not wait to join ***our*** organization, and it went like that night after night.

Our team name, *TNT*, was often mistaken as a sign of ***our*** powerful recruitment of business partners. But, in fact, the origin of the name was a Bible story that Tommy would often tell when invited to speak at churches, which he had done for many years prior to becoming involved in the business.

In three of the gospels in the Bible (Matthew, Mark, and Luke), was revealed a mighty miracle where Jesus healed a woman with an "issue of blood" (uncontrollable female hemorrhaging). The climax of the story details how the woman touched the hem of Jesus' garment, and his "dunamis" was released. "Dunamis," translated from Greek, comes from "dunamai" (where the word dynamite comes from), and means force, miraculous and inherent power. Thus the birth of *Team TNT* (aka God's power). This was Tommy's brainchild, and we would always publicly share that

God was the reason for our miraculous success in the business in which we had no experience.

With the explosive growth of the team, we soon set-up camp at our mentor's home and were joined by my son, Shon, BFF Ronda, college roommate Kathy, and my girl Beverly, to assist with the influx of new reps. With bodies, laptops, cellphones, training manuals, legal pads, and clothes sprawled out in every corner of the house, the estate resembled a 24-hour call center.

Shortly after that, we had similar setups in New York run by our cousins Debra and Lisa; also in Georgia, led by my sister Evelyn with my mom assisting, with Tommy, Shon, and I traveling back and forth to encourage the teams.

It was a common occurrence for us to visit prospects on their lunch breaks, kid's practices, the train station, or the unemployment office. We were not ashamed to hand out flyers at the mall, in parking lots, or *Starbucks* while picking up a chai latte.

While this hectic pace would have been difficult for the average person, it took an even more extreme toll on my body, especially since I'd been diagnosed with a rare form of thyroid disease years earlier. My fatigue weighed me down so much it felt like I was carrying a 300-pound Sumo wrestler on my back.

I'd never used my extreme exhaustion as a crutch before, and I didn't want to begin. It was imperative I led by example. I'd learned early in life; people would only do one-tenth of what they see their leaders do. If I slacked off, it would put a damper on the momentum we were having and the lives of the everyday people we were changing.

In only 14 days, Tommy had broken an 11-year company record by hitting the position of National Director (ND). I could not stop now. Our entire team rallied around Tommy to help him break another historic record by achieving the esteemed position of Senior Vice President (SVP) in just 85 days.

We were ecstatic! We celebrated for all of 30 seconds before returning to the grind, to continue pounding the phones, hitting the pavement, and packing out dens and living rooms with eager prospects. The momentum was out of this world, and our team was hitting the top of company charts with ease, causing amazement.

What made this achievement all-the-more impressive was the fact that all of our success was rising on the heels of one of the worst recessions ever.

TNT had grown to over 500 strong in months. People were reaching out to us via *Facebook*, *Twitter*, and text to join our fledgling network marketing organization. It was incredible! The word was out about the crazy attorney who was shutting down his thriving law practice and his general sister who held the troops together. We were doing national calls and posted flyers around the entire city.

In the midst of all the celebrating, I was thrown a curve ball when I learned Rick's former boss, the lady who called the office requesting that I drop the charges against my attacker, called the law firm looking for me. A few hours later I'd received an urgent text message from the office saying Rick called the office requesting legal services from Tommy.

Since I knew I was still in danger, I never went anywhere alone. I was always in groups with Tommy, Ronda, Kathy, and Bev, but primarily my son. Shon was my guardian angel. A mother could not ask for a more protective son. At only 21 years of age, he watched over me like he was in U.S. Special Forces. While updating the district attorney's Office about Rick's violation of the restraining order, I received a blocked call. Expecting a new prospect, I was infuriated when I heard the caller say, "Denair, this is Kelly, Rick's former boss."

She continued by saying, "I'm interested in joining the business and I wanted to get your take on things. I understand you and your brother are doing quite well." "Really?" I thought, and responded with a CLICK. "How did she get this new number? Oh man", it dawned on me. We had been doing national conference calls, radio spots, and posting info on flyers all around the country, especially in Maryland. I never thought Rick would try *this* angle!

I immediately put a halt to all campaigns that included my whereabouts and contact number. Tommy thought I was going overboard, but complied to appease me.

I assumed Rick might be monitoring my activities, setting up his next attack. Everyone seemed to think I was overreacting, but my suspicions were confirmed two days later while attending a gathering of 800 reps at the *Greenbelt Marriott*. I noticed Kelly sitting directly behind me when I turned around. She casually greeted me and congratulated me on my success. I calmly walked away looking for Tommy, but he left my side to meet guests as the meeting had concluded.

I couldn't spot anyone on my team. No Shon, Bev, or Ronda! I began panting heavily as I feared Rick was nearby. As I scurried looking for my crew, I asked myself if this was really a coincidence.

In a county of 881,000 people, and a room of 800, what was the probability she'd be just eight-inches from the back of my head?

As I located Tommy, trying to tell him of my concern, my imminent danger, it was of no use! He was locked into closing our guests. I slipped out a side door of the hotel and frantically zigzagged the parking lot searching for my car in the dark. I was ducking behind cars, avoiding being spotted by Rick, whom I believed to be close by.

I drove around in circles for the next three hours. I was a mess!

I called the district attorney's office at 7:59 a.m. to report the three incidents of contact by Rick. My assigned victim's advocate did not seem concerned and said to keep her office posted if I noticed anything else. I was outraged! Wasn't the prosecutor supposed to be protecting the people? I *was* the people, but it didn't seem to matter, and certainly did not feel protected.

In the next few days, we were scheduled to travel to the national convention in New Orleans, Louisiana. This is the largest gathering the company held, connecting individuals from around the country and beyond. My trip to New Orleans was in five days and under no circumstances would I leave the house without my entourage.

Finally, landing in New Orleans gave me a little solace. I would be out of the grips of my attacker and his cohorts. On day one of the convention, *TNT* was on the map! Unbelievably, *TNT* reps swept nine consecutive awards for production. This was unheard of, considering 99% of the team had no prior multilevel selling experience. Chants of "T-N-T!" echoed throughout the New Orleans Super Dome. The arena, which was at the epicenter of such great despair and pain a few years earlier, was now hosting *TNT*'s breakout success.

In the midst of celebrating at a jammed packed, all white-party, I turned around to see Rick's best friend staring directly into my eyes, fewer than five feet away. My good vibe was swallowed up my anger.

This time, when I alerted Tommy, he was quite concerned as well. It was kind of hard to keep passing things off as a coincidence, especially when there were nearly 15,000 people at this event.

I asked myself, "Why here? Why now? Why her?" And the all-important question was, "Is Rick around?"

Tommy rallied some of the team and escorted me to the hotel room.

The next morning represented a new beginning for me. So I put on my *flyest* outfit, four-inch heels, and the biggest smile in my arsenal. I was armed with the prayer, "Lord cover me today because I know you have not given me the spirit of fear. Amen."

Just as the company was announcing promotions that set the jam-packed arena on fire with excitement, I could feel eyes on me like I was a target. And just then I turned around, and a few rows back, amid all the radiant faces, were a pair of piercing eyes focusing in on me.

Tommy was in arm's length of me as I pulled him in close to try to speak above the rousing crowd. As soon as the finale was complete, as I tried to make it out through the crowds around us, Tommy spotted Kelly and went over to speak with her.

I stayed clear, as I knew my excitement would not make for a good exchange. Whatever she was saying to him seemed to relax his body language, and he shortly took a seat with her as he repeatedly nodded in silence.

The next thing I knew he was walking over to me and asked me to hear her side, proclaiming it was all a huge misunderstanding.

In a calm and collected manner, she said, "I really don't know who you are." I screamed, "You're lying! You know *exactly* who I am! I met you six months ago with Rick at a party at your home!" She said, "I barely know him; he was a random guest."

I reminded her he was in the VIP section at her invitation-only event. "Unbeknownst to you," I said, "for weeks I listened on speakerphone as Rick helped you plan the event."

I shouted, "You're lying! You've called my office numerous times! I've been in the car with Rick and heard you guys chatting it up. He always told me you guys were the best of friends. Now you're claiming you barely know him?"

Being the psychologist that she was, she hit Tommy with, "It seems your sister may need counseling. Have you tried counseling, sweetie?" She calmly turned to me while shaking her head back and forth as she continued to say I might possibly have post-traumatic stress disorder (PTSD).

I was two-seconds from putting my foot through her lying mouth before Tommy told me I was making a scene!

For me, the convention ended on a sour note. I vowed to spend as little time in Maryland as possible. True to my word, upon my return to Prince George's County, I began my ongoing road trips to support *TNT*, away from Maryland. Members were spread around the country.

As I crisscrossed the United States, I was blown away by the number of friends, family members, and complete strangers who were joining our team via the Internet and live PBRs. Families who were formerly struggling financially and on the verge of divorce now had a little extra cash to splurge on each other.

God was guiding our steps. I was incredibly grateful for His grace and mercies!

By this time, Tommy was sporting his brand new 2012 5-Series BMW, and 5,000 shares of stock, compliments of the company. I was not doing too shabby myself, expanding to about 1,000 reps in my down line. Team *TNT* as a whole was shattering records, with many of us on the verge of becoming SVPs too.

It typically took even overachieving, hard-running, peakperforming reps, anywhere from 18 to 24 months to achieve this position, and we were running like our lives depended on it.

As I traveled hours, days, and nights, driving to various remote locations, I coached our fearless reps on how to recruit *up*. Remarkably, we went from recruiting minimum wage earners to having a huge percentage of our team being comprised of doctors, lawyers, preachers, engineers, professional musicians, realtors, and financial services professionals.

There was one occasion where I had the opportunity to recruit a husband and wife team who were both high six-figure wage earners. Still being relatively new to the industry, I considered handing the meeting over to more qualified representatives. Instead, I said a brief prayer and met with them boldly and confidently. Within an hour, they were both card-carrying members of the *TNT* family. They were very aggressive and acquired new customers and business partners with ease. By day 30, I received an alarming call stating the husband was being downsized at work. His entire department was being outsourced to the Philippines immediately. On day 31, I received a report from the rep who lost his job. His commission check had arrived, and it was nearly double the bi-weekly salary he had just lost. There were many stories like these, including my own, that reminded me of God's "Dunamis!"

By month six, *Team TNT* had grown to well over 20,000 members, and there seemed to be no end to the outpouring of blessings. We'd rise at 5:30 a.m. and pray over blank enrollment forms and travel schedules, hoping the Lord would heed our prayers and bring rapid success to the reps that were joining the team by leaps and bounds.

My obstacles were bringing me closer to God, and I found myself praying more and more with or for others. I'd pray for the team, their families, and their finances, for safe traveling mercies, but mostly I'd pray that Rick wasn't tracking my movements.

As a result of our success, Tommy and I had become semi-celebrities in the network marketing world and within our company. We'd host calls where hundreds of new and experienced reps would tune in to hear our remarkable success.

It was quite common for me to plan my email address, cell phone number, current location, and travel schedule for the next five to seven days.

No matter how many times I omitted my information from the flyer, I would always see an updated version somewhere in cyberspace.

I felt so vulnerable and was always looking over my shoulder and constantly checking my rear-view mirror. My mom would always quote a beautiful Bible verse to me:

"For I know the thoughts that I think toward you, saith the LORD, thoughts of peace, and not of evil, to give you an expected end." (Jeremiah 29:11).

I'd stand in front of audiences of 50-500 complete strangers, and tell them I was an options broker. I'd say, "I'm not here to push some get rich quick scheme; I'm simply here to offer you a plan

B." I'd share how I searched high and low for a job, whose hours corresponded with my kid's daycare schedule. I'd disclose how my grandmother, a very influential woman in New York City, arranged for an interview with her dentist of 30 years for me. I'd recalled how the doctor was extremely charming, spoke highly of grandma, and said he heard I was a reliable, hardworking individual. I'd continue to share how his body language shifted when he said he also heard I had two young kids.

As his smile retreated, he said, "Your kids are not my problem! I don't care whether they have appointments with doctors, school plays, or temperatures of 106 degrees!"

The good doctor ended the interview by saying, "My concern isn't for your children, but for my practice." He straightened up his posture and announced the job was mine if I could make it to the office five days a week at 7:30 a.m. and stay late if needed.

I would take a poll and ask the audience whether they thought I took the job. An overwhelming majority would chant, "No! No! No!" When I confirmed that not only did I take the job, but went on to convince the doctor of my solid family support, the audiences would gasp and almost hiss at me as I would rebut their contempt for my response. I would defensively reply, "And which one of you would let your children go hungry, or even worse, have done the same thing and yet point the finger at me? That's because I, we, are lacking options. Pride went out the window, and my children were sold to the highest bidder. Many of us are guilty. Maybe my employer was more direct during the interview, but honestly", I said, "It's *their* family or yours! And if their children needed new braces, college tuition, and three meals a day, whom do you think your employer would select? Hmm... So again I repeat that I am an options broker, handing out some long overdue benefits."

I forged ahead by telling the audience, "The opportunity you'll hear about this evening literally saved my life. I'd candidly say, "It might be the lifeline you've been seeking as well.

While a large portion of the prospects I spoke to were compelled to lock arms with Team *TNT* financially, a sub group was moved to tears by my testimony. East or west coast, the response was the same; people related to their situation as one that was in need of being rescued.

My initial purpose for doing the business was to make some money to cure my financial situation, which was on life support. I never counted on it being a vehicle to expand my women's ministry. So many women were peeling back the layers that were keeping them from reaching their goals and dreams, just by me pouring into them. As a matter of fact, this part of the meeting would go for an entire hour or more following the business part.

I never questioned why God was using me, a broken vessel, to bless others. I always knew God had a special plan for my life. I didn't know what, though. He anointed my mouth even in the midst of my pain and hiding. Very few of my closest family and friends knew the extent of my invisible scars. I was petrified of being around men I didn't know. I found myself apologizing for things I hadn't done wrong, and I regularly slept with one eye open, or not at all.

Despite the anxiety and fear that was suffocating me, I'd wake up every morning with a burning desire to lead *TNT* to greatness. I'd look forward to basking in their accomplishments and seeing how far they'd stretched outside their comfort zone. I was excited to have birthed a community of achievers who started this opportunity on a part-time basis and many successfully transition to full-time status, over time.

I was completely inundated, but I never missed a beat with the court case. I was showing up to the DA's office with copies of documents, and followed-up with detectives via email and cell. I checked-in with the victim's advocate's office daily and even spoke to officer Gomez a few times a week. I often felt like I was the only one *working the case.* I was obsessed with making sure Rick was held accountable for his crimes against me and the larger society. If I relented, this case, like so many other domestic and intimate partner violence cases would just fade into the background with no hope for justice or peace for the distraught victims.

Rick's attempted murder trial was fewer than 72 hours away. I suspected he'd be up to something, and I was on constant alert.

I'd heard Rick's friend, Kelly, had attended a few business meetings at our mentor's home, hanging out in his inner-circle. There was no telling how manipulative she was. Maybe she'd already discovered I would be landing at BWI on Tuesday morning.

My anxiety was out of control, and everything inside me said not to go to court! I was the only person standing between Rick and his freedom. Against my forebodings, I decided to attend the proceedings. I said, "Lord, please protect me. I know you did not allow me to survive, only to live in fear or die this way." I had to keep encouraging myself in the faith. My mom raised me to believe that God is NOT a man who would lie. I played that *Hello Fear* CD so many times that even when it was off I was still humming and singing. I played it in my car, on my phone, while I was asleep, and when I bathed. I wanted and needed to be so totally immersed in God's promises that even if fear crept in, I would be covered!

6

Joy and Pain!

"Sometimes you have to get knocked down lower than you've ever been, to stand up taller than you ever were." —Unknown

Word spread like wildfire throughout the courthouse!

I could hear the excitement, raised voices, and echoing in the halls.

In the midst of the chaos and confusion, a faint voice chimed in, "He won't get very far!"

There was a sudden rush toward the small room in which I'd been sequestered! The judge had a million questions. He wanted to know whether I had any warning. The perspiration resting on officer Gomez's brow indicated a thousand and one things were racing through his mind.

I thought to myself, "After 218 days and 10 hours, there was finally an urgency for the police, the prosecutor, and court officers to take immediate action. For better or worse, this was the hand I was dealt."

I thought, "Oh! That's reassuring!"

By the time, I'd finally left the courthouse, the story of Rick skipping the trial and forfeiting his $300,000 cash bond was all over the news.

The *CBS Baltimore* affiliate paraded my attacker's mug shot across TV and proclaimed, "Man Charged With Murder is No-Show at Trial.

A man charged with attempted murder of his ex-girlfriend failed to show up at his trial, and police are looking for him."

The *Maryland Gazette* headlines read:

"Attempted Murder Trial Ready; Where's the Suspect?"

Police: "Man beat, choked ex-girlfriend until she passed out."

The *Washington Post* cut right to the chase, simply stating, "Maryland Attempted Murder Suspect Fails to Show at Trial."

I wanted to point and shake my fingers in the prosecutor's face and say, "I told you so!" I could have criticized the judge, who didn't require Rick to wear an ankle bracelet.

I might have even been justified asking why bond was offered in the first place.

Nothing in his sordid past indicated he was a model citizen who'd adhere to the terms of his bond. I suspect the fact he'd fled to NJ after initially trying to kill me wasn't enough. They've put more restrictions on people who sell bootleg movies.

Furthermore, the fact that he attacked a state trooper who was trying to apprehend him after he'd conveniently skipped out on his prior kidnapping case spoke volumes about whether he'd be a flight risk.

I couldn't believe I'd jumped on a 5:30 a.m. flight from Atlanta, only to learn Rick had slipped under the radar again! I'd hoped for a quick verdict and long jail sentence. Unfortunately, the closest person to landing in jail was Rick's attorney, who was playing a dangerous game of *Truth or Dare* with the judge.

The exchange between the two was unbelievable.

Judge to Rick's attorney:

> *Where's your client?*
>
> *Your Honor, I don't know, or least I can't say.*
>
> *Counselor, I need you to divulge your client's whereabouts right now.*
>
> *Your Honor, there's a little thing called* attorney-client *privilege!*
>
> *Mr. Defense Attorney, have you heard from your client or not?*
>
> *Well, Your Honor, yes and no!*

Judge to Defense Attorney:

> *Which one is it?*
>
> *Well, I haven't heard from him directly, per se, Your Honor!*

By now the judge's patience was running thin.

> *Sir, you're 30-seconds from being held in contempt of court.*
>
> *Well, Your Honor, my office did receive a text yesterday from said defendant indicating he wouldn't be joining us in court this morning.*

The judge had had it up to his eyeballs and was ready to explode when the attorney suggested one of the defendant's family members might have suddenly fallen ill or possibly been rushed the emergency room.

Yes, a bench warrant was issued for the thug who attempted to kill me!

Yes, the prosecutor was finally up in arms.

I was absolutely certain that capturing Rick would not be a high priority. It was hard enough getting him back the first time from New Jersey, and he virtually turned himself in by crashing into a government building and passing out drunk at the scene.

If I had any doubt in my mind before, this sealed it for me. Everything, I'd discovered about Rick said he was not going down without a fight.

Rick made it crystal clear; this was a life or death issue – his life or my death. He'd proclaimed no fewer than 100 times that horrific evening that he'd never step foot into another jail.

It was like I was speaking in some another language! No one seemed to understand or take me seriously when I shouted from rooftop to rooftop that Rick said he wasn't going back to jail!

Witnessing the scales of justice tilting off-balance was disappointing. The undeniable truth was the entire criminal justice system had turned a blind eye when it came to domestic and intimate partner violence.

Prior to 1984, most police officers could not legally make a warrantless arrest unless a misdemeanor occurred in the officer's presence. If they didn't see it happen, it didn't exist. Advising the husband or boyfriend to "take a walk around the block" was often the extent of police intervention. I guess that's where Rick was, taking his stroll around the block.

I was determined not to wallow in self-pity and especially not today. I'd always pushed past pain and fear! I've always been brave.

As a dainty 12-year-old, I was very athletic and loved playing sports. I heard the doctor telling my mom, "Denair is a tough cookie." He said I should've been screaming in pain and unable to walk. I had severely fractured my left foot in an accident 10 days earlier. I was afraid to tell because my elder siblings swore me to secrecy since we were not supposed to go outside on this particular day. The doctor was confused as to how I managed to continue running, jumping, and playing on the swollen, deformed foot.

No matter what came my way, I was resilient enough to see it through. Sometimes I'm down, but never out. As I exited the courthouse, my phone chimed, indicating the delivery of that day's motivational quote. "I could use a bit of inspiration right now," I thought as I looked down at the screen.

"Be more splendid, more extraordinary. Use every moment to fill yourself up." —Oprah Winfrey.

I just smiled to myself and said, "Done!"

"Tommy, there is something I want to tell you."

"I'm not scared anymore. Well, I am still scared. I know Rick is somewhere planning something. There's no way he's leaving that $300,000 on the table! There's a strong possibility they're watching right now as we walk to the car. But I can't be shackled by fear. I've got to live my life. I want to win so badly. I want my power back!"

I then said that I knew it sounded crazy but if we jump in the car right now, I can make it to the Hartford, Connecticut meeting and you're going to Brooklyn. He replied, "Dee if you're not up to it, no one would blame you. Today was a rough day for you—for us."

My brother, one of the sharpest litigators in the country, the attorney responsible for facilitating one of the largest mergers in TV history, was completely speechless, that I'd race six and one-half hours to a meeting after being hit with the most devastating news in my life.

Although I'd been up since 3 a.m., hopped on a flight at 5:30 a.m., and carried an unbearable weight in court for three hours, I found myself saying, "I can! I will! I must!" Interestingly enough, this is something I'd been teaching my infant grandbaby. It was absolutely time to break-up with my fears for good *this* time.

The entire *Team TNT* family had been texting well wishes and prayers of comfort the past few days. I knew if I showed up in Hartford after my strenuous day, the team would really be encouraged and motivated to conquer their own Goliaths. I would often share my testimonies because I believed God used them to bless other people. He would never allow me to go through these trials if He didn't think I was strong enough to make it through.

As Tommy and I sped down I-95, we pulled into *Enterprise* to pick up the rental car. With no time to spare, I accelerated in hopes of dodging the New York City traffic. As I was weaving in and out of traffic, I couldn't help being sarcastic while mocking a line that Tommy recited during his infamous "Get it Done" speech. Unable to get through it without laughing, I said, "This road to financial freedom is not straight; it has roadblocks and miles of traffic." Tommy chimed in and said, "Don't forget it has enemies called New York City potholes." It was good to just let my hair down, at least momentarily. I was excited; I boldly told myself I would quadruple my efforts to build *TNT*. I was passionate about everyone obtaining exceptional success. The idea of dramatically improving the trajectory of their lives propelled me!

After dropping Tommy to his meeting, I still had another 95-miles to go to reach my destination. Upon arrival, the time was so tight I didn't have an extra minute to spare, and the meeting was already in progress. So like Wonder Woman, I changed my clothes right there in the car. I was equipped with my A-game and hoped my testimony would inspire someone hiding their hurt, to walk in their destiny.

I was blown away when I entered the hotel and saw 150 eager guests, lined wall-to-wall in a room designated for 75. I shared my riveting story of how I was down to my last breath when God, in His infinite wisdom, saw fit to rescue me!

I told them, "Today, many of you seated before me are drowning. You're drowning in debt. You're drowning in stress, and at this very moment, many of your lives are spiraling out of control due to a lack of time with your spouse, due to having more month than money, being trapped in your cubicles 50, 60, and 75 hours a week."

I shared with them how I pushed past my personal fears and raced across the country to offer them the same lifeline I extended to 5,000 other members of *Team TNT*.

I shared how my good friend was able to retire from her 15-year career as a registered nurse in fewer than six months because of this opportunity.

I boasted how my 21-year-old son recently signed an enormous deal with a major food chain that would pay him a residual income for many years to come.

I shared how my brother was enjoying five-figure monthly checks and a new 5-Series BMW, after being in business for just 85 short days.

I offered to train them with the same skills I learned from the highest earners in the company. Emphasizing that training builds confidence and confidence builds competence. Ultimately, competence gives them the power to win in this business.

As a result of me pushing past my pain, I couldn't have scripted a more perfect ending. The meeting went off without a hitch, and we had a 100% closing rate. I was so elated and felt completely rejuvenated.

After a grueling commute, I arrived back in New York City at 2:30 a.m. Being the *Energizer Bunny* that I am, I was back up by 6 a.m. hosting our nationwide *Team TNT* worship and prayer call.

For the next 10 days, I was worry-free as I crisscrossed the Northeast, going from homes to hotels introducing stay-at-home moms and overburdened corporate executives to a new formula for lasting wealth creation.

Team TNT was receiving a great deal of acclaim throughout the industry for its astounding growth, and I was ecstatic to have played such a significant a role. The icing on the cake was the call I received informing me I was nominated by *New Vision Magazine*, a major publication in New York City, as being one of the rising visionaries in the city. Eight million people, 500,000 entrepreneurs, and I was selected as being among the best and brightest in the city that never sleeps. Walking the red carpet, having my picture taken by the paparazzi, and being invited to dine with the *Who's Who* at the renowned Eighth Wonder of the World, the Empire State Building, was beyond my wildest imagination.

The letter read:

> *Denair Huggins,*
>
> *Drive, perseverance, ambition, talent, dexterity, compassion, and vision. The individuals we selected are game changers in a post-recession who embraced the synergy of the Obama era and successfully ride the waves of change in the 21st Century. The Movers & Shakers are resilient go-getters. We celebrate their quest for excellence, their "thinktuitiveness" and their dedication to their products, passions, and ideas.*

Wow! I'd joined the ranks with Oprah Winfrey, Daymond John from *ABC*'s *Shark Tank*, and Donald Peebles the largest African-American real estate developer in the United States, being featured in this illustrious magazine.

After 10 days on the road, I returned to Maryland for a little rest and relaxation.

Being away from my family for such long periods of time made me long desperately to see them. Since face-to-face was not an option, I went for the next best thing: Facebook. As my page was opening, a friend suggestion appeared, recommending a possible acquaintance with someone I may want to associate with in cyberspace. I was insulted to see Rick's image as my would-be Internet friend! I didn't want to be his friend in real life! Why in the world would I want to friend him on the Internet?

Just before I hit the ignore button, it dawned on me that Rick never entertained social media. The entire nine months we dated, he barked how he hated those sites. Out of curiosity, I clicked on his profile pic to see where it would lead me. I couldn't believe my eyes. Rick was hiding in plain sight.

Based on his timeline, he'd been posting pictures from Pennsylvania, Virginia, and South Carolina.

He was posting videos by fellow abuser Chris Brown and voicing his concern about violence against young black men. I was in awe, as I continued scrolling through his page. I noticed this hunted fugitive was updating his timeline just about every two hours. And the last location stamp was just three miles from Tommy's house.

The pounding in my head was so severe; it felt like my head was moments from splitting. His audacity was so surreal! He was clearly flipping the police the bird. I called several times and made an unannounced visit to the DA's office. I stopped by the police department as well, explaining what I'd seen. I recommended they pull it up and view it for themselves, to no avail. I finally pleaded with them to check this out. I said that he was using his government name, not an alias. I reported he was driving a blue BMW, pictures of which he posted. I couldn't figure out why no one made a move to check it out.

I'm not an investigator with *CSI* or anything, but wouldn't this be one of the first places you'd look for clues of a criminal's whereabouts? Four days later, the prosecutor finally called me back to say she got my message about a possible lead. When I gave her the details again, she stated that they would check it out, and that was the last I heard from them.

I was convinced Rick was a direct threat to me, even if no one else believed it. I told myself there would be no more fleeing, no more scurrying and hiding in the closet! My goal was to focus all of my efforts on transforming lives while staying alive myself. I was determined to live on my own terms.

As the days went by, I noticed unfamiliar cars idling at the end of Tommy's driveway. I became increasingly jumpy after being followed all the way to the end of Tommy's cul de sac. I knew this wasn't an ordinary passerby because Tommy's house was tucked away in an exclusive community at the end of the street. They would not be *accidentally* turned around for several days in a row. Whoever was lurking outside was there for a particular purpose!

I couldn't believe my ears. I found myself scanning the windows, bracing for an attack.

After sharing my plight with a friend who had a background as an intelligence specialist, within 45-minutes, I had a small team sweeping the neighborhood and the house. Upon gathering intel on my attacker, my associate confirmed my suspicions and expressed concern for my safety. He suggested I quickly relocate or hire a small agency to conduct counter-surveillance.

Really, counter-surveillance and gathering intel were foreign to me. I wasn't in Iraq. I was in Bowie, Maryland for crying out loud! Sensing my apprehension, he leaned forward, looked me directly in the eyes, and said, "Denair, based on everything I uncovered, there's no doubt in my mind, this character is going to rear his head! And went he does, it's going to be ugly."

With my new business steadily growing every week, I couldn't just go underground. Still uncertain about the recommended security measures, I agreed to let the specialist do his job.

Five days after paying my initial retainer to the agency, I'd wondered whether I'd been hustled. There was no patrol car canvassing my neighborhood, no personal escort to and from the bank, and no *men in black* surrounding the perimeter of my meetings.

I was irate at the thought of being taken so easily. Was I that pitiful? I was tired of being a mark! I dialed up my specialist and immediately ripped into him calling him a low-life fraud. Before I had a chance to utter the words "money back," a dial-tone pierced the receiver.

I was so heated I wanted to jump through the phone. "No, he didn't!" Sixty seconds later, I received a startling call from a blocked number. The caller whose voice I didn't recognize told me, I was three-quarters finished with my bran muffin and suggested I shouldn't position myself so close to the rear exit. He went on to disclose my entire itinerary over the past five days. He advised me to get out of this MLM thing immediately and marked me as being the easiest target he'd seen in years.

As this mystery person recapped every single step I'd taken and highlighted my multiple blunders over the past 100 hours, I frantically swung my head left and right trying to identify any spy-like characters. As I circled the restaurant, he urged me to sit down, pay attention, and take notes. I opened a napkin and jotted down the following as instructed:

Denair's 14 Survival Principles:

- Never sit with my back facing the entrance of a restaurant
- Alternate my predictable morning routine and driving routes
- Stay off cellphone and pay attention before entering and exiting my vehicle
- As soon as I walk into a public facility, scan for alternative exits
- Survey restrooms prior to stepping in
- Create an emergency escape strategy as soon as I enter any room
- Only go to gas stations that have high traffic and are well lit
- Never get gas at night, unless absolutely necessary
- Exchange my four-inch pumps for loafers
- Be very careful in large parking lots
- Make daily schedule known to loved ones and check-in periodically
- When leaving the local area, drive and travel with someone else when possible
- He told me to place my cellphone and laptop in a steel cage at night. He told me they act as listening devices. He said any third-rate hacker could watch or listen to any movement in my house when these devices are powered on
- He suggested I resign from *Team TNT* or drastically cut back on my public appearances

The final straw that caught me off guard was the revelation that his guys had identified two individuals who'd been tracking my movements. He said his team was quietly trailing them in hopes it would lead them to Rick.

For years, I'd embraced the acronym, F.E.A.R. (False Evidence Appearing Real). I used it to motivate many audiences at networking functions. However, this time, the threat is real. But I couldn't stand by and be a spectator in life.

Despite the risk relayed to me, I decided to throw caution to the wind and keeping pushing *TNT* to the top

Everything I envisioned in life was right at my fingertips. And besides, I convinced myself it was unthinkable to quit!

Just a few days earlier I felt so empowered, walking the red carpet, being celebrated among the top movers and shakers in the Big Apple, and making the cover of the esteemed *New Vision in Business Magazine*. Living life on the sidelines just wasn't living to me.

I was destined for greatness, and I discovered tenacity within that I didn't know existed.

Even though I had my new security detail in place, I began praying like I never prayed before. I reminisced about the daily morning devotionals my mom held with my four siblings and me. Each day before school; the seeds were planted as I clung to the comforting promises in Psalms 23. These verses had seen me through the most tumultuous times. They were a reminder of God's love and protection.

"Yea, though I walk through the valley of the shadow of death, I will fear no evil: for thou art with me; Thy rod and thy staff they comfort me." (Psalm 23:4).

Although it may seem insignificant to some, this encouraging verse of Scripture kept me from looking like the terrible circumstances I was in.

There were 45 days left before the next national convention in Atlanta for my company! I was working day and night, and would live in my car if necessary, to qualify for the BMW, and earn my 5,000 shares of company stock options.

In anticipation of earning the coveted position of SVP, I penned my acceptance speech 30 days before the convention and with just 100 points to qualify.

The thought of being hoisted 15 feet in the air to be carried in a chair like a queen in front of my family, friends, and 20,000 business partners was enough for my heart to skip a beat. And this is not to mention the passionate speech that customarily followed.

As if my plate were not full enough, I was dealt another shattering blow! While driving my 2006 Nissan Altima from a business meeting in Tennessee, my son was rear-ended while the car was at a complete stop in traffic. Thankful that Shon was okay, my mind automatically shifted to the damage of my mobile office.

Four payments away from paying off my car note, the insurance company alerted me that my Guaranteed Auto Protection (GAP Insurance) had expired just two months prior. How could this be possible when this extra coverage was supposed to safeguard me against this type of tragedy? As I tried to comprehend the ridiculous explanation of why I would not be mailed a check for the full value of my totaled automobile, I must have zoned her out. "Ms. Huggins? Ms. Huggins, are you still there?" I responded with a faint, "Yes," followed by a long sigh as the monotone voice on the other end proceeded.

The estimated damages amounted to $12,000, which exceeded the $8,000 *Kelley Blue Book* value. In short, the car was declared a total loss. After *Nissan* commandeered their balance owed, then sprinkled some other outlandish fees, I was left with a whopping $4,000 to purchase another vehicle. To most this would seem like a blessing, a seamless repairable situation.

Just go down and pick out a brand new 2012 top of the line, something foreign, right? Wrong! There was one huge problem: I was living with the most dreadful credit score. My monstrous FICO score had been haunting me ever since the devastated economy prevented my tenants from paying on-time, and sometimes not at all.

My worst nightmare had caught up with me. "No credit. No car. No business." I surmised. I was expected in New York in fewer than 24-hours, and if I wasn't able to secure a rental car fast, I'd have to tough out the 17-hour trip on *Megabus.*

Instead of pointing the finger at God, I was excited that I'd be able to include this brow-raising obstacle as further proof of how good and merciful He was during the last leg of my SVP push.

Grateful the rental process went through without a hitch, I was back in motion. No time to slow down now. I was all in. However, my thyroid problems were still trying to catch up with me. Fatigued beyond belief, I kept it moving.

While driving at my usual Andre Andretti speeds, I was fully engaged in our morning team prayer call and totally oblivious to the speed traps. Totally caught off-guard by the colorful dancing lights I was abruptly pulled over. I was driving solo and had pulled an all-nighter, anxious to see my ailing mom, and get a good night's rest in my own bed. I had been doing presentations in Miami, Tampa, and Tallahassee for three consecutive days.

Chatting it up with my ear buds tightly nestled into both ears, I did not even hear the blaring sirens. Completed terrified when I realized the blue and silver Georgia trooper was signaling me and was right on my bumper, I peeped down at the speedometer trying to conjure up some sort of defense. As I attempted to slow down, the needle went down as I slowed from 93 to 87 mph.

As I braced myself for the officer's approach, I rehearsed my, "Is there a problem officer?" voice. Before I knew it, a second trooper pulled up that sported a more curvaceous uniform. With a flawless bun and gentle voice, she announced, "Ms. Huggins I'm going to need you to step out of the vehicle and with your permission we would like to conduct a search of your car."

"Was I on *Candid Camera*? Was this some kind of cruel joke?" While being ushered to the side of the road, she continued with, "I have to perform a body search." As she put on her gloves, the next round of questions she fired were, "Do you have any weapons or sharp items on your person?" My *Twilight Zone* moment delayed my response as I fixated on the steady traffic that continued to whiz by. With a blank stare, I finally managed to utter the familiar southern response, "No, ma'am." While the pat-down was taking place, I was able to ascertain that there was an outstanding warrant for missing a court date, which subsequently suspended my license. A ticket that I paid a few months prior had not been properly registered and updated with the Georgia Department of Motor Vehicles.

Although I had documentation in my glove compartment confirming the initial fine had been satisfied, the baritone six-foot, three-inch trooper's muffled voice, and lowered head told me it was irrelevant. He reluctantly parted his lips and declared, "We have to take you down to the station, Ms. Huggins. Unfortunately, it's out of my hands."

My otherwise clean record and two-piece power designer *Tahari* suit were the only things that saved me from being shackled with the undesirable shiny bracelets (aka handcuffs). As I peered through the metal on the window that caged me like a hardened criminal, I turned away from the button-less doors and faced the steel partition in the cruiser.

Praying the mix-up would be cleared up, I rode to the station in silence.

Although I was being booked, I tried to remain optimistic. As the officers sized me up, they began making small talk. And to their surprise, I was the life of the party. I took the opportunity to pass my business cards around to the arresting officer, chief of police, and desk sergeant.

Two hours later, after posting bond, I received a call from the desk sergeant who excitedly proclaimed, "I'm pleased to announce you're speaking to your newest business partner."

I faked myself out into thinking I was in *no ways tired*, but my blood work didn't lie.

The truth of the matter was every time I arrived in Atlanta; I'd rush to visit my personal physician who adjusted the dose of my thyroid medicine. Without the right number of milligrams, I'd be flat on my back, unable to function at full throttle, like a car stuck in neutral. Whenever I was in that position, I felt like I was loaded down with two Sumo wrestlers on top of me. To everyone else I looked perfectly healthy. Thank God I didn't look like what I've been through.

I couldn't stop now. People were watching me, and I was so close to my goal. I wanted to show everyone that if *I* could hit the esteemed position of SVP, *anyone* could. Yes, it was hard work, but I was already working hard, except I was not achieving my goals and dreams.

This grind was not just for me. I was representing so many other women who truly needed a breakthrough. To show them that a single mother of two, battered and abused, extremely fatigued and broken, could also be a testament of nurturing and protecting a long overdue dream, which would pay-off. If everything I had gone through could just help (one) somebody, then my living would not be in vain.

No regrets, no shortcuts, and no excuses was my motto. I just wanted to provide a blueprint that I would be proud of, and in the process, be inspirational and transformational to others who needed to see unlikely success achieved. The roadmap was for women like my daughter, Danika, also a survivor of abuse or, Kathy, my girlfriend from college. It could bring hope to Tammy, a single mother of four, or even Bev, an overqualified, brilliant attorney who struggled to find a great paying job.

The days leading up to me achieving the position of SVP were like a circus act with me balancing the most crucial and sensitive matters of my life. It all seemed to happen at once, with each "breaking news" issue demanding 2,000% of my attention.

Team members who were short on cash, but loaded with possibilities were coming to stay at my home, traveling from all around the country. Calls were flooding in from Alabama to Detroit saying, "I heard you have a little extra space at your house, can I crash at your place? And by the way, I may have one or two other people with me."

In addition to getting *Denair's Bed and Bath* ready, I was still meeting with prospects and acquiring the last customers needed around the clock, which at times were very unconventional. While making a quick run to the local *Wal-Mart* to pick up toiletries for my approaching houseguests, I got a call from the state's attorney's office giving me an update on a Rick sighting. I was so engaged in the conversation; I must have walked up and down the aisles for 20 minutes just to locate the familiar shelf where the *Scott Tissue* was.

Due to the delay, I was now running behind for a one-on-one

appointment I set up at *Starbucks* 15-minutes away. While I was on the phone with the state's attorney's office, a blocked number kept calling me, but I did not want to interrupt my call. Then a series of text messages came through indicating it was the prospect that I was en route to meet. With no time to spare, if I could get the prospect to agree to meet me at the *Subway* attached to *Wal-Mart* I could still make the meeting instead of dashing across town in Atlanta rush-hour traffic. So I, "Yes...yes...yes...yes," and, "Oh, I understand(ed)," my way off that call and quickly called my prospect to make the change.

If all went as planned, I could still make it to *Lenox Mall* in Buckhead to pick up my formal dress for the SVP dinner that I was not yet officially invited to.

It was my birthday, and nothing would do my heart better than to hit the position of SVP on this day. I was only 32 points away from breaking through the glass ceiling. The countdown was in motion. This major accomplishment would increase momentum, not just for *Team TNT*, but also for the entire company and industry of direct sales. It would solidify for other women that were broken, burnt out, overworked, underappreciated, and working their fingers to the bone, but still not making ends meet, that there was something better!

This feat was also for accomplished women that were financially stable, with savings and college funds secured for their children. However, they still encountered the pitfall of lack of time, which is just as deadly as the lack of funds. I had been both at some point or another and wanted moms to attend school plays without fretting over a pink slip on their desk when they returned. Women should never have to play Russian Roulette with their children's health because they have run out of vacation days and send a child to school when clearly the thermometer indicates otherwise.

This significant achievement would serve to show everyone that you don't have to be a practicing successful attorney for 16 years with a huge network to achieve success. Being a successful attorney was not how my incredible brother, Tommy, broke the company record with no experience, although it had become the word on the street. Anyone with the desire to win and the willingness to be taught could, and would win in this business, regardless of background.

Our team was laser focused on collectively instilling the overarching principle that the key component to winning in this industry was faith, vision, hard work, sacrifice, passion, resilience, and the simply, "enough is enough" mentality. Winning is not predicated on how many letters were behind your name like, "ESQ," which graced Tommy's John Hancock. *Team TNT* would set the record straight that a divorced, girl from the housing projects, single mother of two, who was an on-again/off-again college student working multiple jobs could become SVP too!

There were many other women just like me who needed someone to show them that it could be done. They needed permission to dream again and stop abandoning themselves. I accepted the challenge and *had* to see this through for all of us.

According to the corporate office, I had a 48-hour deadline to get them my *Mary Mary* remix theme music ready for the big day. This Atlanta International Convention Center crowd would be the audience to witness me taking off my shackles so I could finally dance. My mind could not conceive anything else.

So my team and I just kept grinding, reviewing the products and services with family members, neighbors, friends, and strangers. Although we were making unbelievable progress, the system was delayed in updating my real-time stats. This meant we had to triple our efforts, but we were prepared to race the clock down to the very last second. This included limited eating, sleeping, and bathing to, like Tommy always said, "Get it Done!"

Operation *Get Denair Across the Stage* was a full-blown, cross-country effort. This was no one-woman show, and I must admit that many people were pushing to get me across the stage, especially my NDs, which happened to be my cousin Debra in New York and my sister Evelyn in Atlanta. My son Shon was the real all-star. Wise beyond his years, he set up an entire base camp in my home to keep everything flowing.

Carried to the Stage

I held onto my royal throne for dear life, as I was hoisted 15 feet above a multitude of powerful, well-dressed, successful, and wealthy entrepreneurs. The burst of excitement, cheers, and rousing applause filled the massive Georgia World Congress Center, Atlanta's world-renowned convention center. Yes, this must be it! All my life I dreamed of this day, without knowing how or when this moment would arrive.

As a child, I would have the same dream, year-after-year. Not one single detail would change during the recurrent dream. I would be fabulously dressed, standing behind a presidential podium, speaking to a sea of people. There were too many faces to count, and no one stood out from the other. The bright spotlight that illuminated my silhouette indicated I was the keynote speaker. This was definitely the right place, the right time, and, undeniably, the right location to be presented to the world.

One of the stately co-founder's announced, "And now, for our final senior vice president. She has been a part of this organization for nine months. She formerly worked with her brother at his law office. She believes that blessings are not blessings until you pass them on. Her greatest inspiration is to be an example to others, especially to women and show them that anything is possible. Please help me welcome to the stage, from the states of Georgia, Maryland, and originally from New York, Denair Marie Felder-Huggins!"

As I tried to maintain my composure and my smile, I was sincerely humbled, grateful, and a little nervous. Although this was a very emotional day for me, there was no time for tears, especially since my incredible make-up and hair stylist, my daughter, Denika, told me it was a no-no. I had to stay focused as the words to my speech were looped in my mind. Both of my freshly manicured, clammy hands were squeezed tightly to the sides of my royal chair. There were thousands and thousands of smiling faces. This was it; the defining moment that would finally allow me to fulfill the dream I began having at the tender age of six.

7

Principles for Success: Mind, Body, and Spirit

Throughout the years, I have been asked how was I able to become so successful and remain focused during the most challenging periods in my life. I must admit, there is no particular recipe cures the ills of life when going through a storm. However, success is a culmination of principles that are applied to prepare, support, and enhance personal development while on your journey to success.

The principles that have been a catalyst for success during my peaks and valleys are fundamental practices aligning the mind, body, and spirit.

Mind

In this world full of technology that requires you to download new software, music, and apps to our devices, it is critical that you are constantly downloading behaviors that promote success to your mind. Programming success can be challenging when there are so many negative influences that subconsciously run counter to your desire. Your mindset must be intentional about success. Download all the qualities into your mind that equate to success. Here are a few things you can incorporate into your daily activity to that end:

- **Read books** that reinforce your goals. Also, select books that will inspire the transformation of your life. Challenge yourself to read one new book a month (that's only 12 books a year). Read a minimum of one-hour a day. There's nothing like the old-fashioned flipping of pages and marking them up with a highlighter
- **Write a list** that celebrates who you are and whom you want to become. Your list can include such power phrases as "I am smart. I am courageous. I am resourceful. I am a great parent. I am a great speaker. I am a winner," etc.
- **Listen to positive music** that affirms success. Your mind responds to the commands it hears. Music affects your emotions and facial expressions and dictates your personality. If you hear just a few bars of music, it can determine if you will be happy or sad
- **Watching TV** too much can actually change your brain in negative ways. Your mind can be over-stimulated from the shows you watch. Sometimes TV can discourage your success by influencing negative behaviors such as smoking, drinking,

doing illegal drugs, and sexually immoral behavior. If you must watch TV, try to watch informative programming and good, clean humor.

Body

Your body often senses when things are right or wrong. Pursuing your objectives will lead you to success even if you encounter setbacks. Physical health means being in good condition, being active, and eating the right nutritious foods. When your body feels good your energy levels will increase, your confidence will get a boost, and your overall health will improve, which are all vital to success.

- **Exercise** stimulates the discipline for success. It also releases chemicals known as endorphins, which reduce harmful stress levels and respond with greater clarity. Low-impact workouts are fine and are easier on your body if you are not into higher impact exercises. Exercise supports a healthy heart. So commit to a routine for at least three days a week for no fewer than 30 minutes per day. I encourage walking, swimming, and bike riding. Whatever your choice, *Just Do It*!
- **Sleep** is a precious gift often ignored and considered overrated. Our rigorous schedules push us to the limit, and although you may be able to function on fewer than the required six to eight hours, you cannot trick your body for long. Sleep relieves many physical and emotional problems. To prepare for a good night's rest, make sure your room is dark, quiet, and has a comfortable temperature. I know it's difficult, but power down

your cell phone, computer, television, and other devices, for a good night's rest

- **Eating** food that is healthy for your body can also save you money. Eliminate fast food from your diet as it tricks your body into feeling satisfied with ingredients high in fats and loaded with sugar. Introduce your taste buds to a more natural diet infusing more fruits, raw nuts, and vegetables. Smoothies are really great during this transition. Let's work on eating to live, and not merely living to eat
- **Water** is at the center of life. This is why no one can live more than three to five days without it. To get the most out of your workday, your brain cells require a delicate balance of water to operate, and when you lose too much water, that balance is disrupted. Your brain cells lose efficiency. Try drinking at least 64 ounces of water a day. This is called the 8X8 rule and is very easy to remember. Build-up to this and keep pushing for your own health. Your success depends on it!

Spirit: Tuning in to God

Spirit is the element in humanity, which gives us the ability to have an intimate relationship with God. I believe that strong faith affects us physically. There are significant health benefits to prayer, as an example. Communicating with God and meditating on Bible verses help people to live healthier, longer lives. Prayer is an outlet for stress and anxiety. Blood pressure can improve. Recovery after surgery is shown to improve significantly in those who find comfort in God.

But prayer is so much more than a therapeutic exercise. Praying to

God is talking to and connecting with the Creator of the universe. You are invited to pray. God Himself invites you to bring your burdens, cares and needs to Him. He even invites you to come boldly in order to find mercy and grace to help in your times of need. He designed you to be in communication with Him, even when it involves success in your personal and professional life.

These simple, fundamental principles have been treasured in my life, and I pray they can benefit you as well, as you strive to reach your goals and dreams.

8

One Video

I reached up, extending my arm as far as it could go, but I still couldn't reach it. I tried again, only this time, on my tippy toes. Hmm...I still can't reach it! More determined, I ran to the kitchen and pulled out a stool, and thought maybe that would work, but I was still not close enough. "I'll try one final time," I thought, unwilling to be defeated. With both hands, I lifted the six-foot ladder that was in the basement. I set it in place, took the first step, then the second, using all my might to make it quickly to the top. I felt excitement welling up as I was getting closer and closer. I was confident this time I would be close enough to touch it, grab it, secure it, and never let it go. I had finally reached my dream.

Although our dreams often seem out of reach, and too high to obtain; sometimes we just need a little assistance, momentum, and motivation to grasp them. That's how it was for me to writing this book. My dream of becoming an author had been shelved because of health issues, financial setbacks, housing situations, caring for family members in need, and the threat of death.

Then one day it happened. One video is all it took. One video made it impossible to leave my dream and book, which I shelved, one more day. So I wiped off my old, dusty, fragile composition notebook, which now had bent up corners. Upon these pages on which I shared my life back in 2005, my story was now ready to be completed. Reluctantly, I looked back at some experiences I had already penned as I laughed, smiled, and almost shed a tear, wondering why I let it sit so long. One video inspired me to tell my story and join the conversation of a silent epidemic—domestic violence. It was a complete eye opener to me and, and I would imagine, the rest of the world.

On September 8, 2014, *TMZ* showed a 30-second clip of the five-foot, eight-inch, 220-pound Raynell (Ray) Rice, running back for the *Baltimore Ravens* initially spitting in the face of his then finance, delivering two brain-rattling left-handed blows to the face. The second punch was so powerful that it sent Janay crashing to the floor after bouncing her head on a metal railing, rendering her unconscious! Equally as devastating was the aftermath that sparked national discussions.

The rolling cameras, like a Hollywood film, captured the gritty details in and outside the elevator. *TMZ* obtained the jaw-dropping footage from hotel security and aired the incident. Within minutes of *TMZ* airing the video, it went viral.

It was quickly circulated to *ESPN*, *CNN*, *Fox News*, and every other major cable network and social media outlet.

All eyes were transfixed by the obvious, undeniable beating that Ray Rice inflicted upon Janay. What was not so apparent was if Janay was a victim of abuse or if Ray Rice was the victim because the video was interrupting his influx of endorsements and football career. To be honest, I don't even believe Janay believed she was a victim of abuse, or at least she could not admit it, because of the pressure imposed on her by the *National Football League (NFL)*.

Commissioner of the *NFL*, Roger Goodell, had originally restricted Rice from two games after being informed of the running back's horrifying deed. However, once the video exposed the full-blown actions of Rice, and subsequently the action (or lack thereof) the *NFL* showed related to one of their star players, Goodell quickly changed his tune. The media attention shifted Rice's two-game penalty to a more severe punishment, which banned him for life from playing in the *League*.

As I watched, the comments of all the respected commentators around the country and even took notice of those I was close to, chime in on the topic, I was ashamed to hear remarks like, "Just let him play," or "He didn't hurt anyone," or "She had it coming," or "She got arrested too." To add insult to injury, Ray Rice held a press conference and apologized to the *NFL*, the media, his fans, supporters, and those whom he endorsed products for, and neglected to apologize to Janay. During the same interview, Janay took responsibility for the role she played in her assault. Janay later admitted that *NFL* strategized her appearances and statement.

A league of well-dressed, highly-paid men had no sympathy for what Janay was going through but rather were more concerned about what the gruesome video footage would do to their pockets, ratings, and endorsements.

The more I followed and researched this story, was the more I encountered the massive cover-ups the *NFL* and other major sports leagues had on similar issues. It became crystal clear how this one video changed the outcome related to this issue.

One sports figure that was very vocal during this period was Floyd Mayweather, Jr. who chimed it with, "A lot worst things go on in people's households. It's just not caught on video if that's safe to say." He continued with, "Like I've said in the past, no bumps, no bruises, no nothing. With O.J. and Nicole, you seen pictures. With Chris Brown and Rihanna, you seen pictures. With (Chad) Ochocinco and Evelyn, you seen pictures. You guys have yet to see any pictures of a battered woman, a woman who says she was kicked and beaten (by Mayweather). So I just live my life and try to stay positive, and try to become a better person each and every day." Shaking my head, I was blown away after listening to Mayweather trying to convince himself of his innocence.

Mayweather, considered the greatest boxer of his era, undefeated as a professional and a five-division world champion, won 12 world titles and the lineal championship in four different weight classes. Unfortunately, Mayweather fights outside of the ring as well.

Here is his record: Seven alleged assaults committed against five different women that resulted in him either being arrested or issued a citation. Also, his former fiancée, Shantel Jackson, filed a civil lawsuit including claims of battery, false imprisonment, and allegations that the fighter pointed a gun at her. In a separate incident, two of Mayweather's children witnessed their mother, Josie Hill, being beaten as he threatened them so they would not seek help. One son disobeyed and notified security of the outrageous crime that was taking place. In all of this, Mayweather still insists, "No proof. No pictures. No crime." Mayweather's facing up to 34 years in prison. He took a plea deal on many of his domestic abuse charges and was released 30 days early for good behavior during his 90-day sentence.

Sadly, just a few months later, the public still supported Mayweather on May 5, 2012, with the largest single-fight purse in boxing history. He walked away with a whopping $32 million from viewers watching the fight on *HBO Pay-Per-View*.

This one video has shed light on the dark shadows of abuse, causing the President of the United States to speak out against it and officially seal it with a Presidential Proclamation—*National Domestic Violence Awareness Month*, 2015. Although the first *Domestic Violence Awareness Month* was observed in October 1987, it had never been acknowledged by another president before Barack Obama.

The message seems to be loud and clear, but the takeaway by many is: "Just don't get caught on video!"

Two years prior to this one video, the lives of Kasandra Michelle Perkins and her three-month-old baby were taken by another *NFL* athlete, Jovan Belcher, who played for the *Kansas City Chiefs*. Belcher, in a hysterical state, shares his crime with Chiefs' general manager, head coach, and linebackers' coach, after which he takes his own life on the grounds of the Chiefs' practice facility. Three bodies, 11 shots to his victims, and one to himself, and surprisingly, there wasn't any change in the *League's* domestic violence policy.

If the *NFL* had implemented a zero tolerance lifetime penalty immediately after the death of Ms. Perkins, there's a very real possibility we may have never witnessed Janay Palmer's unconscious body being dragged out of an elevator.

I looked at Janay Palmer's lifeless body as if it were mine. I cried, thinking that's exactly how I must have looked after my ex-boyfriend tried to kill me; sprawled out, vulnerable, and about to die. As I faded into unconsciousness, I imagined the white chalk outline around my body.

After watching the extended video, I realized that Janay had also been arrested on that night. Apparently officers thought she caused an imminent threat to Rice. Eventually, charges were dropped against her.

I could imagine the guilt, embarrassment, fear, loneliness, and shame she felt. The world was weighing in on her personal issue. The shock of viewing the video and seeing herself lying unconscious must have been overwhelming. The interviews, media comments and her family falling apart had to have made terrible matters even worse. Months after the incident, the couple got married. Now as Janay *Rice*, she is criticized for staying with her abuser. Although Janay paid a horrendous price, I believe that much good can come as a result of this toxic and sadistic video surfacing.

Since the Ray Rice tape was released, dignitaries and politicians alike have spoken out forcefully for harsher penalties for abusers. Twelve members of the House Judiciary Committee also stepped up and spoke out against weak policies. Many other laws around the country and the world have been changed because of this one video.

Here are just a few of the changes. Some laws now:

- Allow victims to testify via closed-circuit television enabling them to confront their abusers without fear
- Allow courts to admit the restraining orders into evidence to determine "whether the use of force was justifiable" if someone is charged with attacking his or her abuser
- Allow victims to obtain restraining orders against perpetrators when no demonstrable personal relationship between the two parties exists, such as when the attacker is a stranger or a casual acquaintance
- Require police to search a registry of domestic violence restraining orders when conducting an arrest

While there has been an incredible outpouring of support, there have still been a few utterly disgusting comments by celebrities that reinforced that we have a long way to go to eradicate the stigma of being a victim.

NBA All-Star, Paul George told his 900,000 twitter followers, "I don't condone hitting women or think it's cool BUT if SHE ain't trippin then I ain't trippin. Lets keep it movin lol let that man play!" (referring to Ray Rice)

George later clarified his statement by adding, "If you in a relationship and a woman hit you first and attacking YOU, Then you obviously ain't beatin HER. Homie made A bad choice! #StayUp"

In other headline news, this one video had a possible impact on another domestic violence case. United States District Judge, Mark Fuller, who was allegedly heard on a 911 recording, kicking, punching and slapping his wife, would have escaped without penalty. He simply had the rotten luck of having his plea agreement of six months of anger management hit the paper the same week of the Ray Rice incident. Mrs. Fuller's screams of, "He's beating on me! Please help me!" captured by 911 really didn't amount to a hill of beans.

The fact that "Police later discovered blood in the bathroom on the tub," did little to sway the judge's, judge. His record, similarly to Ray Rice's, will be expunged if he isn't caught on 911 abusing his wife again. Despite this story being widely covered on *CNN* and numerous other cable news networks, this federal judge will remain on the bench for life unless impeached by Congress.

The conversations swelled throughout many other communities, and I feel compelled to include some of the positive feedback.

Joe Torre, Baseball Hall of Famer and former manager of the *New York Yankees* said:

> *Ray Rice knocking his then-fiancée unconscious with a single punch accomplished one good thing: the footage ripped off the cloak of secrecy that typically emboldens domestic abusers.*

In one of several tweets, including one in which he said Rice belongs in prison, not on an *NFL* football field, Terrance Knighton, *NFL* defensive tackle, *Denver Broncos* said:

> *This video makes me sick to my stomach.*

LeCharles Bentley, *NFL* center, *New Orleans Saints* (retired) said:

> *He could've killed that girl. They need to sports science the force of that punch. NFL players are STRONG... Like very strong.*

London Fletcher, *NFL* linebacker, *Buffalo Bills* (retired) said:

> *To say you got that wrong is an understatement. Very disappointed in you. Wow...unbelievable.*

Jason Whitten, *NFL* tight end, *Dallas Cowboys* said:

> *That's unacceptable. Not only in the NFL as professional athletes but just as men in this world.*

Mike Rawlings, Mayor of Dallas, Texas

> *We should not be looking to Roger Goodell. We should be looking at ourselves...What do we say in locker rooms? What do we say at bars? How do we act? This should be a moment of self-reflection.*

As a result of this one video, hundreds of horrific stories of domestic violence have been highlighted on *CNN*, *ESPN*, *Fox News*, *ABC*, *CBS*, etc. Mayors, governors, and special prosecutors have broken their silence and committed to delivering more resources to victims, pressing for stiffer penalties on abusers and rewriting Pre-Trial Intervention (PTI) that simply gives abusers a free pass to further maim.

More than shaming the *NFL* and its billion dollar empire, this one video will be the force behind thousands of new community outreach programs around the country, new *Blog Talk Radio* podcasts, and other Internet shows that spotlight violence against woman.

More importantly, it will silence the chorus of abusers who have paraded the slogan "NO Pictures... No Proof!"

Although heartbreaking, the prevailing mood of society over the past 30 years has sadly been, "Hear no evil. See no evil. Speak no evil. Not in my house. Not my problem. It's in the past. It's gone!"

9

Why I Stayed

As I recalled an interview where Janay Rice was asked why she stayed, I drifted off reminiscing about the years I encountered abuse in my own marriage. I remembered tuning out before Janay could fully reply. I pulled the cover tightly around my body to prepare for the barrage of criticism. Even though for me, it has almost been two decades, the sting of many of the open wounds ooze pus and need healing.

The non-stop, piercing cries of my three-month-old daughter bounced off the walls of that five-story Bronx walk up, which was supposed to be home sweet home. Denika was caught in the middle of her hostile 20-year-old father, and her baffled, antagonized 19-year-old mother. A progressive argument intensified that sparked the moment my husband at the time crossed the threshold.

In an attempt to ignore and tune out the frivolous argument, I aggressively rushed to the kitchen to get the items needed to bake my legendary mac and cheese. It was to be served as one of the main courses at Mom's house immediately following the baby blessing of our bundle of joy. The hardwood floors creaked as the unwelcomed, angry footsteps closely followed me. With my mind focused on the task before me, I diverted my full attention to my checklist and continued dumping seasonings and other groceries into the *Key Food* plastic shopping bags.

My nonchalant demeanor infuriated my husband rather than doused the flames. I honestly attributed the insignificant agitation to just another intense day at *Montefiore's Neurology* operating room. It was all-too-common for my ex-husband to work long, strenuous hours on his feet as a new surgical technologist without breaks or lunch. The unpredictable, relentless routine would cause him to pass out from sheer exhaustion when he would walk through the door. With our marriage just a few months older than our infant, I figured it was simply growing pangs related to all the new responsibilities he had recently embraced. His modest income was the primary source of support for our instant family.

The decision for me to be a full-time, stay-at-home mom was initially my ex-husband's idea, which I accepted for the wellbeing of our family. We agreed that our primary focus would be to create an environment that fostered nurturing principles and stability for our toddler. Aside from me squeezing in hair clients from-time-to-time to support the family budget, Denika had all of my attention and was lavished with learning games, songs, and activities even at this early stage.

I wasn't a victim. I fought back, or at least I did my best. I wasn't told this was abuse. No one shouted; no one pull me to the side and said, "Run." No hand brought me to a precinct and demanded I file a complaint. No one told me this thing, the control, would mount and continue until I didn't even recognize myself.

I'd watched Robin Givens stand by her man on *Barbara Walters*. She took the blame. I'd watched Whitney Houston proclaim Bobby Brown was the sweetest thing since sliced bread. While rumors swirled around, she was being viciously abused. My landlady and church member told me, "That's the way things have been, and that's how it'll always be."

Similarly, reading Janay Rice's *Instagram* and public support of her husband reminded me of how I also felt responsible for the abuse I experienced. Many terrible things he shared with me about his past led me to believe he had a troubled upbringing. I wanted to believe that our relationship would be different, and *our* family would be better off together, someday, eventually, after a while. However, that day never came. Progressively, not all at once, things got worse-and-worse.

As I travel the country and hear the stories of many survivors and some still living with their abusers, each story has many dynamics.

We often put ourselves in the place of the victims and imagine ourselves leaving at the first signs of abuse. But breaking free of abuse is not merely a matter of walking out the door. Leaving is a process.

It can be difficult for many people to understand why a person would stay in an abusive relationship. But there are many reasons. Strong emotional and psychological forces keep the victim tied to the abuser. Sometimes realities like a lack of money prevent the victim from leaving. The reasons for staying vary from one victim to the next, and they usually involve many factors.

In my relationship with Rick, I didn't immediately recognize his controlling nature. When I did, I *tried* to distance myself from him. I initially blamed his ongoing questioning on my grueling work schedule and not being engaged enough in the relationship. When he confided that he, too, had been viciously beaten by his wheelchair-bound mother who blamed him for her unhappiness, I thought a change of environment was what he needed to pacify his insecurities.

"You are so stupid! You should just leave! That would never happen to me! She deserves it then! If that was me..."

These are just some of the compassionless comments that rang in my ears after I escaped and announced that I had been in an abusive marriage for almost 10 years. The taunting, probing, and unapologetic banter I endured mimics the suspicious overtone that keeps countless victims silent and cemented in their abuse.

Why did *I* stay? That is simple the question. But honestly, the answer is *not* as simple. I'm sure most people are familiar with the classic textbook responses such as, "I was in constant fear. He said he would kill me. I will hunt you down. I will hurt your family. If you leave, I will kill myself." Well, these answers did not apply to me. To be completely honest, I was not afraid of him at all.

I did not see myself as a victim at the time. I had a reputation for fighting growing up. I was never a bully, but I never walked away when boxed in a corner either. But these were serious crimes. I wanted to help him heal. I thought fighting back meant I was strong, but it just broke me down, slowly but surely.

10

Make Over Mansions

"It has been said, 'time heals all wounds.' I do not agree. The wounds remain. In time, the mind, protecting its sanity, covers them with scar tissue and the pain lessens. But it is never gone."
—Rose Kennedy

I hated living in a shelter, and I'm never going back! My mind cringed as I reflected on my sixth-grade school year, which was one of the worst times for our family. Our once beautiful, inviting, two-story, brick home was now a mere shell of its former self. The palace where I laid my head for the past 11 years had been declared uninhabitable.

Our fascinating six-foot aquarium that was lined with decorative gravel, driftwood, and swaying green plants, was now one huge block of solid ice. The freezing temperatures inside the home were a result of neglected bills that were months behind.

These conditions forced my family and me to relocate to even worse conditions in the 104th Street shelter in New York City. I never wanted to see that place again, let alone take my children to a place like that for protection. This is the image I had of all shelters: rat infested, bed bug ridden, slimy unsavory neighbors who want to rob you at any given opportunity.

My vision for makeover mansions would encompass all the tools for assisting survivors with the resources needed for total restoration. A beautiful home surrounded by grass and trees, not a dilapidated, rundown environment. Counseling for all victims, including children whose scars seem to go unnoticed. Continuing education for victims who need better employment opportunities and relocation funds to those who need to leave the state to start fresh, away from their abuser. This one may seem insignificant, but a new wardrobe and hairdo are things that can help rebuild the confidence of someone who has been stripped of their dignity and self-esteem. These are all things that I was lacking.

Many times victims are left feeling disheveled, displaced; mentally, emotionally, and financially crippled. It takes them years to take on the title of survivor and scramble to adapt to their new lives, oftentimes, and not receiving child support because of the angered, detached spouse. Feeling they are inflicting pain on the adult, manipulative abusers grasp their last stronghold of power and withhold finances needed to support their children. Sadly the abuse does not end when one party leaves. It can morph into many forms, including stalking.

11

The Prayer Call

"Put your shoes way under the bed at night so you gotta get on your knees in the morning." —Denzel Washington

"No weapon that is formed against thee shall prosper..." (Isaiah 54:17). This Bible verse in a vacuum could not deliver me from the ills of life. However reaffirming your faith, actually *claiming* God's promises, and praying is a great formula for starting your day on the right foot.

I woke up at 6 a.m. with a burning desire to just fall on my knees and thank God for another chance to breathe. Breathing, this simple physiological process, taking air into the lungs and then expelling it is a luxury that most of us take for granted.

This function was strangled out of me just two months prior to my brother Thomas, many of our team members, and I begging God to bless a national prayer call that would reach thousands (our church without walls). This sanctuary saved my life in a tremendous way.

Prior to September 24, 2011, my life was full of joy, laughter, determination, ambition, spontaneity, self-confidence, being task-oriented, and laser-focused. Almost overnight I became fragile, distant, reserved, anxious, distracted, emotional, and afraid of my own shadow. I even found myself sleeping behind the couch curled up in a ball.

It truly blessed the lives of many who needed an outlet of this magnitude. However, the person whom it blessed the most was me! I was in desperate need of restoration and new life.

"And the LORD God formed man of the dust of the ground, and breathed into his nostrils the breath of life; and man became a living soul." (Genesis 2:7). That is *my* testimony. God breathed into my nostrils, and I became a living soul again.

There are no words adequate to thank God. There is no payment I can give Him. I can only honor Him. And what better way can I honor Him than to give Him glory every single day as soon as I wake up?

The *TNT* worship and prayer call, as it is affectionately called, takes place seven days a week. Each day, there is a specific theme led by a broad range of facilitators, including pastors, counselors, health professionals, as well as listeners of all age groups.

Each day, we dial into a toll-free number to worship God through uplifting, motivating praise reports, testimonies, Bible stories, and of course, prayer. This is not like any other prayer call you have ever experienced. It is the funniest, most electrifying, spiritual, energetic group of worshipers you have ever encountered.

I often say that the *Steve Harvey Morning Show* ain't got nothing on us. They have competition. Yes, this prayer call helps people breathe life into their situations that may look hopeless and dismal.

My mind races to gospel recording artist, Byron Cage, and a song that he sings that melodically describes how honored I am to be in God's holy presence at the beginning of each new day.

This is the air I breathe

This is the air I breathe

Your holy presence living in me

This is my daily bread

This is my daily bread

Your very word spoken to me

And I I'm desperate for you

And I I'm lost without you

What a precious gift. God gave me the ability to inhale and exhale through all the things that were weighing me down. The opportunity to give God back the first fruits of my day, together with those I love the most, is something I was raised to do since I was a toddler. I am thankful for my mother's obedience and example. She instilled this great appreciation to worship as soon as I get up. Before turning on the television, before listening to the weather, before checking traffic, or even before checking my phone for text messages I worship. With the psalmist, David, "I will lift up mine eyes unto the hills, From whence cometh my help. My help cometh from the LORD, Which made heaven and earth." (Psalm 121:1–2).

Not only did the Lord make heaven and earth, but he also made the amazing *Team TNT*. *Team TNT* is comprised of some of the most diligent, passionate, committed individuals around the country. Most of us knew we could not take credit for the tremendous success the team was having in our new business venture that was allowing dozens, then hundreds, to retire from their traditional nine-to-five jobs.

One of the most significant days on our prayer call is Thursday; this is a platform for me to have some of the most intimate discussions with women, including domestic and intimate partner abuse. Yes, we allow women, men, and clergy to express their experiences they encounter, but most importantly I try to guide them to leave these situations safely.

12

Having an Exit Plan

When you reach your tipping point and feel the need to run for *your* life, and away from your abuser, it's important to consider the following when developing a safety plan. Safety plans evolve over time and with the severity of danger, which can change very quickly. There are certainly no one-size fits all safety plans. It's important to assemble information about your local organizations that have up-to-date information and resources that are available to you.

There are different safety plans or combinations thereof depending on the situation. For instance:

- Consider safety planning when no one leaves
- The batterer has left or has been excluded from the home
- The survivor is planning to leave

- The survivor has left (and may return several times before leaving for good)
- When the survivor has left permanently or has relocated

*Note that violence can increase when the abusive partner is losing control over the victim/survivor.

Here Are Some Safety Tips:

- Consider a code system that you and your children can use to alert neighboring family or friends that you are experiencing abuse
- Create a paper trail by reporting and journaling your experience
- An order protection *may* be an option to keep a distance from the abusive partner, but in some cases can exacerbate the violence. It's important to determine if it is safe to obtain one
- It's strongly encouraged to work with your local domestic and sexual violence organizations to develop your safety plans and be informed of the services available to you

Back to New York

This time, I was running *toward* God's plan for my life.

It's been almost 20 years from the time I literally escaped from New York until now. I have come full-circle and have run right back to the belly of the beast. But now I ran to a new beginning, my destiny to bless and change the lives of women who were just like me. I ran to help women who were abused, but it did not look like it. I ran to help women who have children, hopes, and dreams but have lost their way, self-esteem, and courage. This is what led me to return to the city that I vowed I would never, ever go back to, especially not to live.

I currently sit on the executive board of one of the most dedicated domestic violence organizations in the country—*CONNECT: Safe Families, Peaceful Communities.*

CONNECT is a non-profit organization in New York City that is dedicated to ending intimate partner and family violence. By building partnerships with individuals and communities, *CONNECT* strives to change the beliefs, behaviors, and institutions that perpetuate violence. Through legal empowerment, transformative education, and community mobilization, *CONNECT* seeks to create safe families and peaceful communities, and ultimately, eradicate violence against woman and girls.

CONNECT was among the first anti-violence organizations in New York City to recruit men as allies in ending violence against women and to engage diverse faith communities with long-term work around domestic violence and child abuse.

CONNECT has been so impactful that other countries have requested their training to end domestic violence, such as Italy, Kenya, Thailand, Paris, India, and South Africa, just to name a few. Closer to home, *CONNECT* has included our men and boys to become allies and activists in ending domestic violence; in particular, their Annual Father's Day Pledge against domestic and intimate partner violence, held at New York's City Hall.

Domestic and intimate partner violence is a worldwide issue. It does not discriminate by social class, ethnicity, education level, or age. If you want to learn more about how to become part of the solution feel free to contact *CONNECT* directly for additional information. *CONNECT* is solely supported by donations, and I urge you to give a donation as well.

The sale of this book will contribute to *CONNECT's* worldwide cause, so give one as a gift to further the work already begun. Your support matters! Thank you.

Visit http://www.connectnyc.org/ or for:

General Inquiries

Phone: 212-683-0015

Email: connect@connectnyc.org

Legal Advocacy Helpline

Monday-Friday | 9:30 a.m. to 5 p.m.

Phone: 212-683-0605

About the Author

Denair Marie is an advocate and educator that empowers women, youth, clergy, and corporations around the country. An animated and riveting storyteller, Denair's keynote talk titled, "Converting Obstacles to Opportunities," is so powerful and wonderfully delivered, it often evokes tears of joy and standing ovations.

Denair's book, ***Run for Your Life***, is an intriguing cat and mouse tale of how an aspiring attorney, fled her dream job and her amazing new home. Denair ran for her life after her ex-boyfriend, who was charged with her attempted murder, jumped bond and led federal marshals on a harrowing chase. Her abuser used intimidation tactics trying to discourage her from testifying.

Denair is an award-winning entrepreneur who has delivered hundreds of presentations to Chambers of Commerce, women's roundtables, and aspiring entrepreneurs.

Although Denair had every reason to give up and give in after the collapse of her real estate empire:

5 – surgeries that left her nearly bed ridden for years

4 – generations of domestic violence that wreaked havoc on her daughter, granddaughter, and mother who had been stabbed 60 times; and Denair being strangled and beaten within inches of her life...

3 – violent car accidents

2 – personal bankruptcies

1 – arrest after being a victim of domestic violence

Despite the ugliness and pain that left her destitute, she rebounded to become a very successful entrepreneur. Her home-based business strategies are setting trends around the country. Her trademark brand, *Living Room Wealth* is making it possible for women to create generational wealth from the comfort of their homes.

Denair's 12-year ministry includes mentoring, coaching, and a hands-on approach in community work. *Sister's Table Talk*, a national prayer line, enables her daily inspirational words to reach those who have been battered and bruised. It is engaging, fresh, and a springboard towards healing.

Denair is currently an executive board member of *CONNECT Safe Families NYC*. *CONNECT* is dedicated to preventing inter-personal violence and promoting gender justice. *CONNECT* strives to help change the beliefs, behaviors and institutions that perpetuate violence. Through legal empowerment, grassroots mobilization, and transformative education, *CONNECT* seeks to create safe families and peaceful communities.

For more information about Denair or to book her to speak at your event, visit: www.denairmarie.com

65658760R00120

Made in the USA
Charleston, SC
28 December 2016